MARKETING TO THE ENTITLED CONSUMER

FOREWORD BY **STEVE YOUNG**, NFL HALL OF FAMER

MARKETING TO THE ENTITLED CONSUMER

HOW *to* TURN UNREASONABLE EXPECTATIONS *into* **LASTING RELATIONSHIPS**

Nick Worth & Dave Frankland

with Josh Bernoff

www.mascotbooks.com

Marketing to the Entitled Consumer

For more information, please contact:
Mascot Books
620 Herndon Parkway #320
Herndon, VA 20170
info@mascotbooks.com

Library of Congress Control Number: 2018907119

CPSIA Code: PBANG0818A
ISBN-13: 978-1-68401-559-7

Printed in the United States

To Angela, Sean Luca, and Shaw

CONTENTS

FOREWORD

by Steve Young

When Dave and Nick asked me to write this introduction, my first instinct was to decline. I'm a businessman, investor, broadcaster, and retired quarterback, not a marketer. What could I add? They pressed me, asked me to read their draft, and pointed out some parallels from some things that I had shared with them about my experiences on the football field.

In my NFL career, I threw 107 interceptions. One hundred and seven times, I dropped back to pass and threw the ball to the other team. I don't remember every single one, but each one was painful. And each time, all ten of my teammates on the field would look back at me and ask, "Why? Why did you throw the ball to the other team? We trusted you. Of all the things you could have done, why did you throw it to them?" Meanwhile, 60,000 people are jeering you in the stands, and you still have to walk to the sideline and face the coach.

What do you do? You try to explain it. After all, it's not like I dropped back and meant to throw it to the other team. So I'd list the reasons: the sun was in my eyes, the ball was wet, the guy hit me just as I was throwing, the receiver was supposed to go left but went right—there was always a reason. But the coach didn't want to hear it. And my teammates would just shake their heads and say, "Steve Young...he can't quite cut it in this league."

I learned that in that moment you have to take accountability. Right then. In the moment. I learned to turn around and say, "You know what? I screwed up. But I tell you what—let's get the ball back, go down the other end of the field, and win the game." And the dynamics changed. We'd go to the sidelines after an interception, and the coach would ask what happened. And then one of our offensive linemen would say, "Well, coach, I let the guy get inside me, and he hit Steve just as he was throwing the ball." Or the receiver would say, "I turned left but was supposed to turn the other way." Suddenly, we were in it together. Accountability and collective responsibility became infused into the system. Something must have worked because we went on to win a lot of football games after that.

I've found that this works in every aspect of my life. Now, when there's a problem, I try to identify it, take ownership, and figure out how to fix it. And if you're a marketer today, you're probably aware that you have a problem. You're throwing a lot of interceptions every day and every week—sending irrelevant offers, bombarding consumers with retargeting messages for items that they have already purchased, or sending competing messages and offers in different channels.

And just like handling a wet ball or having the sun in your eyes, there are plenty of excuses you can point to. Data is scattered in places throughout your company, making it hard to get a complete view of an individual consumer. Your business is divided into separate units that communicate independently with customers, meaning they get all manner of competing messages. Or your communication systems across email, text messages, your website, etc. aren't designed to integrate with each other, so it's hard to sync up your marketing activities.

But here's the problem. As Dave and Nick show in *Marketing to the Entitled Consumer*, today's consumers are like the best coaches—they're not interested in your excuses. And like the best coaches, if you don't improve, they'll replace you. They'll take their business elsewhere in a heartbeat if you can't deliver the kinds of experiences that they expect.

So what can you do? Just as I learned after one too many interceptions, you have to recognize the problem and take responsibility. And that's what Dave and Nick will help you to do throughout this book: identify the challenges with marketing to entitled consumers, and figure out the approaches you can adopt to help turn those unreasonable expectations into lasting relationships.

Steve Young is co-founder and managing director of the investment firm HGCC and chairman of five of its portfolio companies. He was inducted into the Pro Football Hall of Fame after a 15-year professional football career including two most valuable player awards and three Super Bowl Championships with the San Francisco 49ers.

PART 1

THE CASE FOR CONSUMER-FIRST MARKETING

WHAT DO WE KNOW ABOUT GENERATION Z, SO THAT WE CAN GET THEM TO BUY STUFF?
SO FAR, ALL WE KNOW IS THAT THEY HATE BRANDS THAT TRY TO GET THEM TO BUY STUFF.
TOM FISH BURNE
© marketoonist.com

Chapter 1

UNREASONABLE EXPECTATIONS

We're going to start with a little story. This story is about you, or could be. And everything in this story is true, or could be.

In our story, you live in Los Angeles, and it's time for you to fly to Paris.[1]

You walk out the door with your bags and tap to order an Uber. As usual, it arrives in three minutes.[2]

In the back of the car, you launch Skype and connect with your friend who is spending the summer in France. You see her smile as you tell her when you'll be arriving. The call is free. She reminds you that you owe her a few dollars. You Venmo it to her with a couple of taps on your phone.

When you get to the airport, your boarding pass pops up automatically, and you use it to sail through security. And you're off.

The point is not how amazing these things are. *The point is that they are commonplace.* People move rapidly from enjoying new capabilities, to expecting them, to counting on them. Now, if they break, we get mad. Imagine telling somebody from five years ago that you no longer need to go to the ATM to deposit a check or take out a credit card to pay for something. They'd be amazed. Now, if Apple Pay fails and you need to dig out the credit card, then you feel that Apple and the merchant have let you down.

When we raise the topic of entitled consumers, we often hear negative feedback about Millennials. Young people seem entitled to so many services, especially in places like Silicon Valley, that residents have described the local lifestyle as "assisted living for Millennials." But as you'll see from our research, it's not just Millennials who feel entitled. A sense of entitlement is rapidly spreading to all of us, all over the world.

We, the consumers, spend little time reflecting on how good we have it now. In fact, we always want more.

We complain that the little black car on the Uber screen lags the actual location of the car picking us up, sometimes by several blocks. We complain at the checkout when the credit card with the chip takes ten whole seconds to get approved. And lord help us if Amazon takes more than two days to deliver something, even if the shipping is free.

Face it. We're all entitled consumers.[3] And we're getting more entitled every day. We live with previously unimaginable levels of service and convenience, and our only response is to ask for more.

This book is about two things.

First, it will help you to understand the breadth and depth of this entitled attitude—what it is, who has it, how they feel, and what they expect.

And second, it will help you to embrace and profit from it.

THE FEELING OF ENTITLEMENT IS ACCELERATING

Consumers now expect you to provide an ever-increasing level of service and customer experience—and for free, if possible. Take a look at what's already possible and what's coming (see table 1).

Table 1: Emerging interactions that fuel a sense of entitlement

INDUSTRY	COMMON NOW	EMERGING
Financial services	Pay a friend instantly with Zelle.	Savings automatically invest according to your risk profile and needs.
Telecom	Make a call to anybody anywhere, including video, for free.	To change your service, you just tell the telecom company's chatbot.
Grocery	Blue Apron delivers fresh ingredients for a whole meal.	Samsung refrigerator orders food when you're running low.[4]
Travel	Hipmunk finds you the flights that minimize cost and travel hassle.	Sleep in your autonomous car as it drives between cities.
Media	Watch a whole new season of shows the day they come out.	Shows that you'd like find you on any device.
Retail	Wave your phone to check out.	Pay automatically as you walk out the door without stopping at the register.
Apparel	Virtually try on clothes to see how they look at Uniqlo.	Clothes that you'd like arrive at your door, and you can send them back after a few months.

If your industry is on this list, the expectations are rising. Even if it isn't, these sorts of experiences are making people feel entitled. As a marketer or supplier, you don't just compete with your fellow retailers, or travel companies, or manufacturers. You live in a world of entitlement.

It's the Amazon effect. Dominant online retailers like Amazon set expectations with infinite selection, competitive prices, and fast and free delivery. Consumers bring those same expectations to every company they deal with, as you can see from the quote on this page from a guy named Will who participated in one of our focus groups. As Jim Davis, VP of global omnichannel marketing at Deckers, the footwear company that owns megabrands UGG and Teva, told us, "Amazon is constantly overdelivering. It forces other businesses to do the same. They expect delivery—and returns—at the pace of Amazon."

"Amazon is the standard you judge others by. I feel safer on Amazon; I have more experience with it."

WILL, customer service rep, US

These expectations spread to every industry. Steve Furman, the director of digital customer experience for deposits at the financial services company Discover Financial, has been carefully tracking consumer behavior for two decades. As he observed, "Consumers are projecting onto financial services many of the things they get in retail and the sharing economy."

When we encounter an experience we enjoy, we learn to count on it. Then we expect all other companies to step up and deliver the same experience. Then, as we begin to rely on it, we become disappointed when other providers don't step up to offer it. Experiences we have with one company set our expectations for other companies, even those in other industries. This phenomenon is so widespread that we have a name for it: the transference of entitlement. (We'll describe it in more detail in chapter 6.)

In 2017, we surveyed 7,000 people: 2,000 in the United States and 1,000 each in France, Germany, Italy, Spain, and the United Kingdom. Fifty percent of them expect companies to provide free shipping. And 43% want to be able to return anything they get without penalty. (We also conducted focus groups in four different countries—you can see some of the comments from the focus group participants on these pages.)

"I get annoyed if [companies] make me pay for the delivery [and free returns]. One that gets me really mad is when I have to print out the return label. I have to print it at work and then bring it back home, and it's just annoying."

CHRISTINA, PR director, Germany

According to future-focused analyst Jeremiah Owyang, founding partner of Kaleido Insights, 90% of the things you buy are about to be digitally enabled and connected. We're talking baby bottles that tell you when they're empty, washing machines that order detergent when they run out, and earbuds that block annoying sounds, amplify important ones, and translate languages.

Whatever these experiences are, we will always want more. It's not enough to just stream Facebook and email to an airplane at 30,000 feet. We're not happy just because we can connect in a metal tube going 500 miles per hour five miles up in the air. No, we need the Wi-Fi to be *faster*.

We want a Zipcar or a Mobike to be waiting for us whenever we need it so that we don't need to own any transportation. We want Rent the Runway to provide us with designer dresses we can wear once and then return.

"Consumers have always wanted good customer service," explains Discover's Steve Furman. "The veil has been lifted on how bad customer service is. The expectation is higher now; people feel like they can vote with their dollars."

Incremental improvements are insufficient. As Steven Van Belleghem, the visionary author of *Customers the Day After Tomorrow,* told us, "The focus is customer-centricity in a world driven by technology. Today, too many companies are trying to incrementally improve what they have. They don't go fast enough. They don't go far enough."

There's a penalty for failing to keep up with these new demands. When we don't get what we want as consumers, we will switch. Forget contracts—if you get sick of your mobile service provider, T-Mobile will buy you out of your contract. If you get sick of Whole Foods, Blue Apron will deliver meal ingredients and instructions right to your house. If you're sitting in the appliance showroom, you can whip out your phone and check if that dishwasher is any good—and if you're not getting the attention you want, see if it's available somewhere else *right now*.

In a study by the customer experience experts at the Temkin Group, only 11% of consumers said they would give brands a second chance if they had a negative experience.[5] And online community provider Lithium's survey found that 49% of US and UK consumers would switch hotel providers after one negative experience, and 41% would switch airlines.[6]

I just hate flying with Ryanair, because their customer service is so poor. [With any brand] there's a limit, and there'll come a point where they'll do something and then I just won't do it. I'll pay more money with another brand, because I won't go with them.

STUART, sales manager, UK

If we don't like what we're getting, we expect to be able to return it without penalty and get something better. And some company, somewhere, will take care of that for us. As every company in the world attempts to live up to those expectations, they are only reinforcing our idea that we are *entitled* to this level of service, and it's only going to get better.

Can your company compete in a world like this? To do so, you'll need to not only deliver what the customer wants but also anticipate it. And that requires something that's often lost in the world of the entitled consumer: a close, familiar relationship between the consumer and the companies serving her.

Companies delivering ever-higher levels of service **REINFORCE** consumers' entitled attitude.

RESTORING FAMILIARITY AND LOYALTY IN A DIGITAL WORLD

Think back, for a moment, to one hundred years ago. You shopped at the local store. The shopkeeper knew whether you were married, had just had a baby, had a weakness for fancy lace, or bought a lot of nutmeg. The shopkeeper knew you. And because he knew what you wanted, you came back. Personal service generated loyalty.

That changed, slowly but steadily. People wanted more choice, and they wanted the goods they chose faster and cheaper. That meant suppliers had to pursue something more compelling than familiarity: scale.

Price competition and the pursuit of scale led to the world we live in now, where everything is mass-produced as cheaply as possible. The corner store has been replaced by Walmart and its massive, efficient global supply chain dedicated to beating prices down to the absolute lowest possible level.

The knowledgeable storekeeper of the nineteenth century was replaced by "marketing"—the science of creating desire efficiently. Even though marketers now collect more information than ever before, they use it to market more efficiently, not to know and serve the customer better. Companies want to move product, stuff channels, and target "cohorts," such as women ages 25 to 44. Companies only know consumers by the target groups to which they belong.

Except for the most exceptional, consumer-focused companies, loyalty is fading—or it's just transactional, a fleeting preference bought with frequent buyer points.

It's time to bring back the familiarity that we've lost, without giving up on the scale that makes everything so cheap and convenient.

You can see the beginning of this swing back to personal service in some of the more advanced suppliers. Companies like Amazon, Netflix, and USAA watch what we do and improve their service based on what they observe. They guess what "people like us" are looking for, and often they're actually right.

The promise here is huge. Because now companies can know everything a consumer does—every click; every time she opens an app; and every purchase, store visit, and piece of media consumed. With the right algorithms in place, companies can efficiently turn this information into a completely personalized experience. This is the next step in serving entitled consumers.

Except for the most exceptional companies, loyalty is FADING—or it's just a fleeting preference bought with frequent buyer points.

And consumers *want* to be known. They like it when Facebook assembles everything they've ever done, munges it in an algorithm, and shows them what they want. They like it when Google searches look different based on everything they've ever searched before. In fact, as our survey data shows, they expect you to market to them. They know you're collecting their data. They'd like you to be smart with it and curate their experience accordingly. And if you do, they'll be just as loyal to you as they are to Facebook and Google.

Your website needs to recognize people. Your call center needs to know their history. Your app needs to show them what they're looking for based on where exactly they're sitting and on the weather around them. And as for store staff, you had better arm them with mobile devices powered with the same personalized information, even as you ensure that your personal service still respects their privacy.

Is this possible? It is now. Today's consumer and marketing technologies make it possible to give consumers the one-to-one, individualized experience that will keep them coming back and to deliver that experience efficiently, at scale. That's what this book is all about.

MEASURING THE TWO DIMENSIONS OF ENTITLEMENT

Entitlement is not just an abstract idea. We can measure it. Analyzing our survey of 7,000 people in six countries on both sides of the Atlantic, we found that in every country, the majority of people feel entitled, act entitled, and expect companies they interact with to give them exactly what they want. Just as you might suspect, the constant ratcheting up of expectations from the likes of Amazon, Apple, and Disney has created a growing mob of entitled consumers.

We were amazed to find that the sense of entitlement was pretty much independent of traditional demographic categories. Baby Boomers (born between 1946 and 1964) were slightly less likely to feel entitled than Millennials (born since 1978) or Gen Xers (born between 1965 and 1977)—but only slightly. Man or woman, rich or poor, college graduate or not, your chances of behaving in an entitled way with the companies you deal with are about the same.

Entitled consumers WANT to be known.

What we did find is that entitlement is measurable and that it's not a one-dimensional phenomenon.

The two dimensions of entitlement

Our analysis of the survey data revealed that entitlement is actually a synthesis of two related qualities. We call them hard entitlement and soft entitlement.

Hard entitlement manifests itself in people making demands. It correlates with people who expect discounts for poor service and demonstrate frustration with companies that abuse the data they have about customers. Consumers who display hard entitlement also expect more control over the methods that companies use to market to them. Their basic attitude is, "If you don't give me what I demand, I'll punish you."

Soft entitlement is related but a little different. It's reflected in people who are willing to share data to get better service and expect companies to understand their needs. These consumers are anticipating better service, but they understand that they'll have to share something with the company to get it. Their attitude is, "I'll help you give me what I want, because that's what I've come to expect."

In every country, the majority of people feel and act entitled, and they expect companies to give them exactly **WHAT THEY WANT.**

You can visualize the two dimensions in the form of a two-by-two matrix (see table 2). At the top right are people who feel both forms of entitlement—we call them Fully Entitled. Those who demonstrate only soft entitlement are Anticipa-

Table 2: Entitlement segments, with percentages of US consumers in each segment

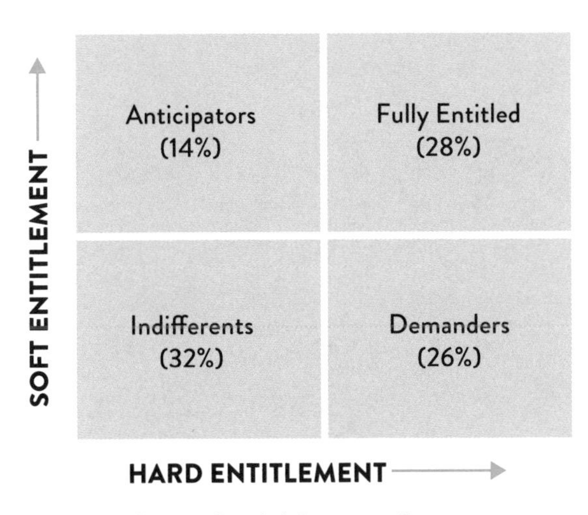

Source: Entitled Consumer Survey.
Base: 2,000 US consumers.

tors, since they anticipate better service in exchange for the data they share. Those who demonstrate only hard entitlement we call Demanders, because they make demands on the companies they work with. And there are still consumers who don't feel any form of entitlement. We call them Indifferents.

As you can see from table 3, 68% of Americans are in one or another of the categories of entitled consumers. These include 28% of American consumers who are already Fully Entitled, demanding what they want and working with companies to get it. Another 14% of American consumers are Anticipators and 26%

Table 3: Entitled consumer segments by country

		ENTITLED CONSUMERS		
% IN EACH SEGMENT	INDIFFERENTS	ANTICIPATORS	DEMANDERS	FULLY ENTITLED
France	39%	13%	29%	20%
Germany	35%	19%	22%	24%
Italy	29%	25%	14%	33%
Spain	20%	15%	21%	44%
United Kingdom	29%	15%	25%	31%
United States	32%	14%	26%	28%

Source: Entitled Consumer Survey.
Base: 2,000 US consumers and 1,000 consumers in each of the five European countries. Note: Totals may not sum to 100% due to rounding.

are Demanders. Only 32% of Americans are Indifferents, who don't display either quality of entitlement—yet.

Since entitled consumers are hard to spot, you have to treat **EVERYBODY** as entitled.

These proportions vary by country, but in every country where we did surveys, the overwhelming majority of consumers feel entitled in some way. There are relatively more Anticipators in Italy. France is the only country where Demanders outnumber the Fully Entitled. But the pattern is very similar: a large group of Fully Entitled consumers, somewhat smaller groups of Anticipators and Demanders, and a lump of more-or-less Indifferent consumers at the bottom.

Entitled consumers are everywhere. How can you spot them?

It's not easy.

After examining every possible demographic characteristic, we found that entitlement is only detectable through attitude and behavior. Entitled consumers may be young or old; men or women; educated and affluent or not; or urban, suburban, or rural. Your traditional marketing cohorts of "men aged 25–34" and "women with college degrees" won't help you identify them.

The conclusion is clear: if around two-thirds of your customers are entitled in some way, and you can't identify them right off, you have to treat everybody as entitled. The Demanders will punish you if you don't, the Anticipators will leave in disappointment, and the Fully Entitled may do both. As a result, you'll have to give them all the highest possible level of personalized service on your site, on their phones, or in your stores. Once you do, as we'll describe in the rest of the book, you'll be able to develop profitable relationships with them. And as we found in our surveys and focus groups, and as history bears out, the Indifferents will be coming along shortly, expecting the same stuff today's entitled consumers want.

Before we leave this topic, here are some snapshots featuring statistics about each of these four segments. The statistics you read here are blended data, reflecting the views of all 7,000 people in our survey from six different countries.

Fully Entitled

Table 4: Percentage of Fully Entitled by country

Country	France	Germany	Italy	Spain	UK	US
% Fully Entitled	20%	24%	33%	44%	31%	28%

Source: Entitled Consumer Survey.
Base: 2,000 US consumers and 1,000 consumers in each of the five European countries.

Both hard and soft entitlement. Fully Entitled consumers:

- *Will work with you and share data but punish you for poor service.*
- *Expect you to tap in to every possible technology to know and serve them.*
- *Will go on social media and trash you or leave a bad review if you don't accommodate their needs.*

Areas where they score higher than all the other segments:

Affinity for technology:

- *"When I encounter a new technology, I can figure it out quickly."* (75%)
- *"I tend to adopt new technology products before my peers."* (45%)
- *"I can't keep up with all the social media posts, email, messaging apps, SMS, etc."* (35%)
- *"I feel stressed when I am separated from the internet or social media."* (33%)

High expectations:

- *"It's shocking how bad companies are at knowing who I am or understanding my needs."* (45%)

Open to relationships with companies:

- *"I look forward to reading messages from my favorite companies, even if I am not looking to buy anything in particular."* (48%)
- *"I love shopping."* (63%)

Want miracles delivered by technology; would be happy if:

- *Airline popped up boarding pass on mobile device when arriving at airport* (71%)
- *Bank or credit card company interrupted when about to buy to point out better pricing elsewhere* (69%)
- *Hotel allowed check-in to room on mobile device without having to go to the reception desk* (65%)
- *Movie theater sent information about the screen location and a refreshments coupon on arrival* (63%)

Figure 1: Fully Entitled consumers expect more from companies

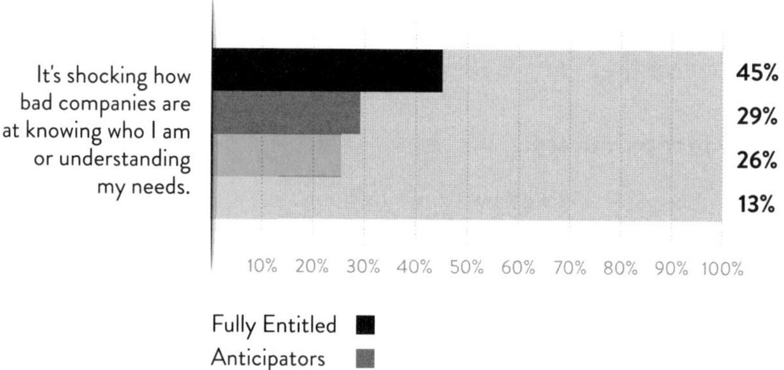

Source: Entitled Consumer Survey.
Base: 7,000 US and European consumers.

Figure 2: Fully Entitled consumers want personalized interactivity

"I would be happy if . . .

% who agree (top two boxes)

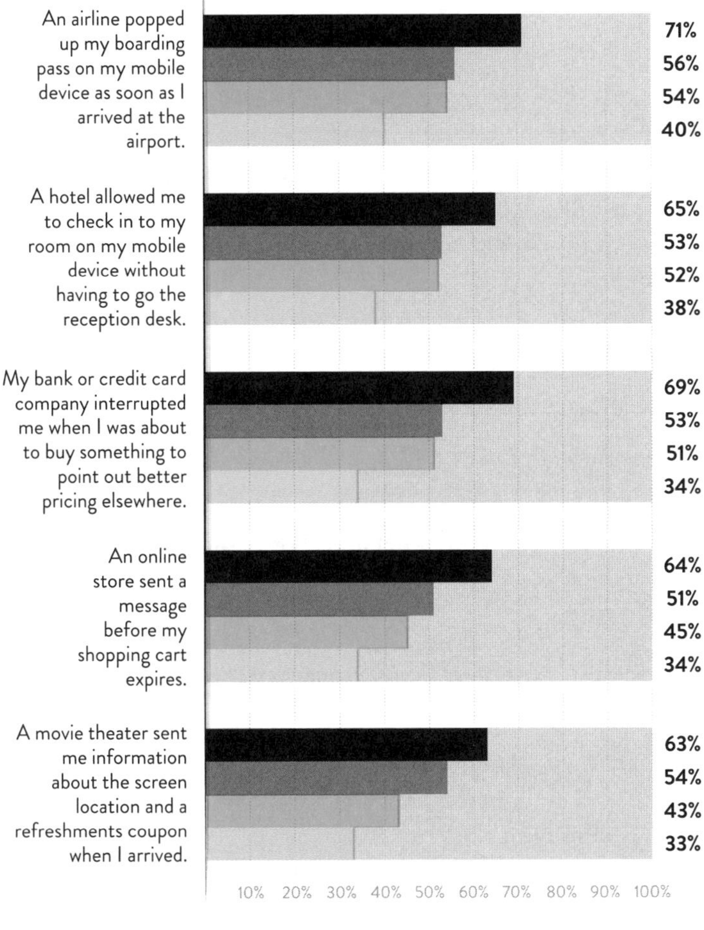

Fully Entitled
Anticipators
Demanders
Indifferents

Source: Entitled Consumer Survey.
Base: 7,000 US and European consumers.

Anticipators

Table 5: Percentage of Anticipators by country

Country	France	Germany	Italy	Spain	UK	US
% Anticipators	13%	19%	25%	15%	15%	14%

Source: Entitled Consumer Survey.
Base: 2,000 US consumers and 1,000 consumers in each of the five European countries.

Soft entitlement only. Anticipators:

- *Would rather work with you to get the best possible service.*
- *Are collaborative but have high expectations.*

Areas where they score higher than all the other segments:

Collaborative:

- *"I read all the messages from companies that I like."* (53%)

Areas where they score nearly as high as Fully Entitled consumers:

Technology affinity:

- *"Companies should use my personal data to provide me with better service"* (81%)
- *"When I encounter a new technology, site, or app, I can usually figure it out quickly."* (69%)
- *"I tend to adopt new technology products before my peers."* (45%)

Positive attitudes toward companies:

- *"I look forward to reading messages from my favorite companies, even if I am not looking to buy anything in particular."* (42%)
- *"I love shopping."* (59%)

Regarding expectations of personal service, if a company gathered their data:

- *Would have much higher expectations of service and/or relevance.* (24%)
- *Would spend time to answer questions to improve the quality of experience.* (23%)
- *Would be more loyal to the company.* (23%)

Figure 3: Anticipators embrace technology and communication

% who agree (top two boxes)

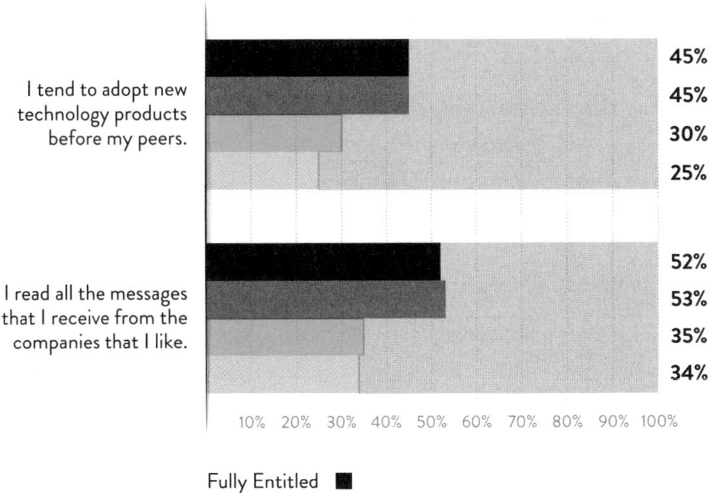

Source: Entitled Consumer Survey.
Base: 7,000 US and European consumers.

Demanders

Table 6: Percentage of Demanders by country

Country	France	Germany	Italy	Spain	UK	US
% Demanders	29%	22%	14%	21%	25%	26%

Source: Entitled Consumer Survey.
Base: 2,000 US consumers and 1,000 consumers in each of the five European countries.

Hard entitlement only. Demanders:

- *Expect a lot.*
- *Are impatient and demanding.*
- *Will punish you if you fail them.*

Areas where they score higher than all the other segments:

Demanding; when purchasing, look for:

- *A competitive price (75%)*
- *Free shipping and returns (55%)*
- *Ability to return product or cancel service without penalty (51%)*

Tend to research before buying:

- *Searched online for a lower price, free shipping, or other perks (58%)*
- *Compared features or prices of competing or similar products (57%)*
- *Read or watched online ratings or reviews by other consumers (44%)*

Punish inadequate service when product doesn't meet expectations:

- *"I return the product and ask for my money back."* (45%)
- *"I tell my friends and family about my negative experience."* (45%)

Suspicious and concerned with:

- *Getting 'hacked' or experiencing a data breach that exposes data* (83%)
- *Sharing consumers' data with other companies* (78%)
- *Tracking location even when consumer is not interacting with company* (76%)
- *Tracking behavior on other companies' websites* (71%)
- *Would avoid company that gathers information to deliver personal service* (39%)

Figure 4: Demanders expect compensation and exact punishment

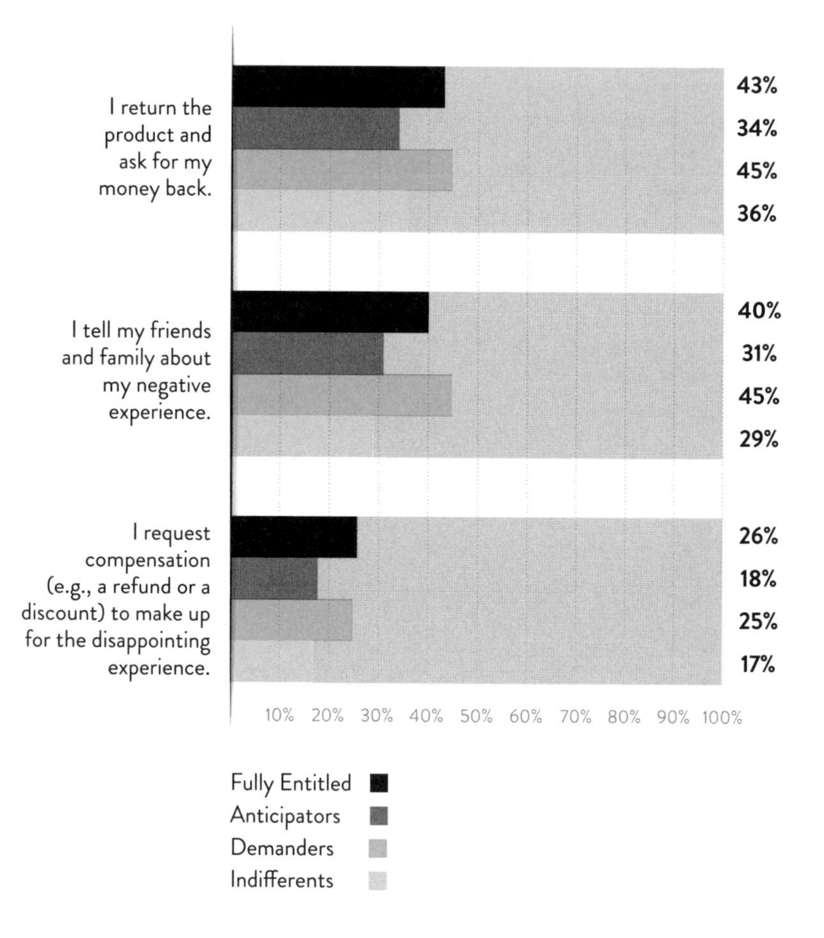

Source: Entitled Consumer Survey.
Base: 7,000 US and European consumers.

Indifferents

Table 7: Percentage of Indifferents by country

Country	France	Germany	Italy	Spain	UK	US
% Indifferents	39%	35%	29%	20%	29%	32%

Source: Entitled Consumer Survey.
Base: 2,000 US consumers and 1,000 consumers in each of the five European countries.

Indifferents are:

- *Not entitled on either dimension.*
- *Apathetic toward companies they buy from.*

Areas where they score lower than all the other segments:

Affinity for technology:

- *"When I encounter a new technology, I can figure it out quickly."* (55%)
- *"I tend to adopt new technology products before my peers."* (25%)
- *"I feel pressure to update my social media on a regular basis."* (10%)

Less demanding of companies:

- *"It's shocking how bad companies are at knowing who I am or understanding my needs."* (13%)
- *"Online shopping has made me less patient when I am physically in an actual store."* (17%)
- *"If I can't get what I want in under 2 minutes, I'm out of there."* (8%)
- *"Companies should use my personal data to provide me with better service."* (12%)

- *"Companies should anticipate my needs and meet them before they arise." (6%)*

Lowest expectations for advanced services; would be happy if:

- *Airline popped up boarding pass on mobile device when arriving at airport (40%)*
- *Bank or credit card company interrupted when about to buy to point out better pricing elsewhere (34%)*
- *Hotel allowed check-in to room on mobile device without having to go to the reception desk (38%)*
- *Movie theater sent information about the screen location and a refreshments coupon on arrival (33%)*

Figure 5: Indifferents have the lowest expectations

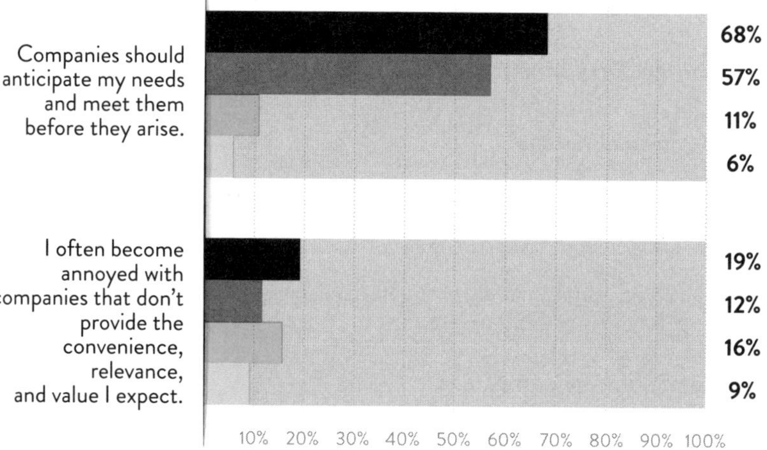

Source: Entitled Consumer Survey.
Base: 7,000 US and European consumers.

WHAT THOSE STATISTICS MEAN

Let's roll this all up for you.

We've now learned that two out of three consumers in America and Europe feel entitled to some extent.

You can ignore how they feel. And that might work for a while. But every company in the marketplace is setting expectations that those two-thirds of consumers are noticing. Free shipping, personalized recommendations, apps that pop up relevant offers when you pass a store, unprompted acts of kindness—that's what they're increasingly getting from the companies they deal with. And that's what they now expect to get from you.

The Demanders are a little more willing to punish you for failing them, while the Anticipators are a little more willing to work with you. But you can satisfy all of them, and the Fully Entitled consumers, by committing to one concept:

Successful marketing to entitled consumers demands that you take everything you know about them and use it to serve them with timely, personalized marketing based on reciprocal value, relevance, and respectful empathy.

To be clear, you must deploy these services *carefully* and only to the extent that customers tolerate them. That one strategy will win over the Demanders, the Anticipators, and the Fully Entitled consumers—and eventually, even the Indifferents will follow along.

To meet the expectations of entitled consumers, companies and their marketing and service organizations must adapt. We must treat every customer interaction as an opportunity to know and serve customers better. Bombarding them with irrelevant offers and messages is not only an-

Two out of three consumers in America and Europe feel **ENTITLED.**

To **MARKET** to entitled consumers, use everything you know about them to deliver timely, personalized marketing based on reciprocal value, relevance, and respectful empathy.

noying, but it will also destroy the crucially valuable relationship that creates ultimate revenue from this entitled customer. We have to recognize that at any given moment of interaction with a customer, she may need to find information, fix a problem, cancel a subscription, or expand her relationship: vastly different needs that require completely different responses. The company's job is to identify that need and solve it as quickly, efficiently, and seamlessly as possible. Do so, and you will make that consumer feel privileged—and you will earn her business for a very long time.

This is much harder than it sounds. It demands a new approach that we call "consumer-first marketing." If your marketing approach is channel-first, or brand-first, or product-first, you will eventually lose. While there are many sources of leverage, a consumer-first approach is increasingly the only approach that will matter. Your competitors are already focusing on how to make their consumer feel entitled. Unless you adapt, consumers will simply leave you.

These days, the consumer is often the last piece of the marketing puzzle—after we've decided which products we're promoting in our fall email campaign, we then do segmentation and selection to determine which consumers should receive it. A consumer-first approach turns this on its head. It requires that we look at the individual consumer, seek to understand the context of her needs, and then consider what is most relevant and valuable to her. This demands that we seek *first* to understand the consumer and *then* to build relationships on her terms—with integrity, empathy, and a concern for the value of the relationship to the consumer.

NOW WE TEACH YOU HOW TO DO IT

Here's what we've included in this book.

In the rest of **Part 1: The Case for Consumer-First Marketing,** we explain how we got to this point and why a consumer-first strategy is the only way forward. This includes what you just read about entitled consumers, plus chapters on marketing overload and the principles of consumer-first marketing.

In **Part 2: The Elements of Consumer-First Marketing,** we show you how to do it. The first two chapters in this part describe how to approach data and omnichannel communication, two prerequisites for making consumer-first marketing work. Next come chapters on the three Rs, the pillars of a consumer-first marketing strategy: reciprocal value, relevance, and respectful empathy.

In **Part 3: The Impact of Consumer-First Marketing,** we take a step back and examine what this new approach to customer engagement means in a broader sense. This begins with a comprehensive chapter on the consumer-first marketing framework, which you can use to evaluate how your company is progressing as it begins to embrace this new way of doing business. We finish the book with a look at how consumer-first marketing is changing the world as more and more companies adopt it.

Throughout all of these sections, we've included case studies, statistics from our survey, quotes from our focus groups, and pointers to highlight key insights. And we end each of the remaining chapters with a list of suggestions on what you can do to embrace the principles of consumer-first marketing.

Treat EVERY customer interaction as an opportunity to know and serve the customer better.

Seek **FIRST** to understand the consumer and **THEN** to build the relationship on her terms.

We've tried to put everything you need into these pages. And we'll get you started with a close look at how entitled consumers are responding to the overwhelming flood of marketing messages they receive every day.

THE CONSUMER-FIRST MARKETER'S TO-DO LIST

We end each chapter with a list of takeaways for marketers. These are your to-dos to prepare your mind for consumer-first marketing:

- ☐ Recognize that consumers' expectations are rising across all sectors and in all geographies because interactions from advanced companies like Amazon make them feel entitled.

- ☐ Understand entitlement as a complex phenomenon that includes both the hope for more personalized service and the willingness to penalize companies that don't deliver it.

Happiness may be found in the open toe sandals you browsed yesterday.
A dream will be fulfilled if you buy the flatscreen TV in your shopping cart.
RETARGETING HAS GOTTEN OUT OF HAND.
TOM FISH BURNE
© marketoonist.com

Chapter 2

MARKETING OVERLOAD

For 28 years, Olivia has been working for a large regional auto club in North America, an organization that provides members with vehicle-related services. Olivia (not her real name) has worked her way up to a management position in digital marketing. She really wants to do the right thing when connecting to her customers, but it's not easy. Like many marketers we've interviewed in all sorts of companies all over the world, she's frustrated.

"There are multiple groups from our organization contacting the customer. We really have no idea what we are sending out to members on any given day," she told us, very plainly annoyed. "They may not even have a membership. They may not even have a car anymore."

Olivia has been with her employer for the entire history of digital marketing. She remembers when the idea of email as a marketing tool was new. Then people realized it could be used to connect with customers. It seemed virtually free. But, as with all effective and inexpensive tools, it got overused.

As an organization, Olivia's auto club has multiple lines of business, from a travel agency to credit cards to insurance and car repair. Each of those business units has its own ideas on what is important. There are travel newsletters, insurance newsletters, and emails that a member gets after receiving emergency roadside service. The digital marketers at the auto club are sending members 16 million emails every year.

And that's not all the communication a member gets. Each time a customer takes her car to a service center, the service center sends a follow-up email. And then, most likely, another, and another. Some of those "reminders" include coupons and suggestions to sign up for other services. Since each center communicates independently, they send those emails without regard for what other communications the member may be getting.

While these emails appear to be free, they have a cost. The auto club, of course, must pay for email service providers, address acquisition, and design. But the real cost of overusing emails is in what it does to the customer relationship.

Here's an example. One day, working with a financial services partner, the auto club sent 150,000 members a solicitation to invest their money in a certificate of deposit (CD). If the member deposited $15,000 in a CD, she'd get a $100 bonus. The offer not only failed, it backfired.

Only 8% of the recipients opened the email. Out of 150,000 recipients, only 22 people invested. That's a conversion rate of just over 0.1%, not surprising given the paltry offer. Olivia estimates the total value of those conversions to the organization was about $4,000.

But every email has a hidden cost in member annoyance. In this mailing, 75 people became sufficiently annoyed to opt out of the email. (That's right, there were more opt-outs than conversions.) The auto club calculates that subscribers on its email list buy $86 per year more in services than other members. They typically continue to engage with the organization for 20 years or more. A conservative estimate, then, is that the auto club lost over $1 million in revenue just from that one misguided mailing.

When it comes time to measure the true cost of marketing overload, that's just the beginning, because every one of those irrelevant offers chips away at the brand. The auto club's brand is local and national. And one by one, its members are beginning to associate it a little less with service and a little more with relentless harassment.

"We just think we can throw these emails out there, not consider cadence, not consider business-line goals. We get greedy, we just start sending things without being smart about it, damaging our brand, and damaging the trust that they've given us," says Olivia. "If you are not doing it right, you will lose [the customer] altogether."

A COMMON TRAGEDY

All over the planet, marketers just like Olivia are doing their jobs as diligently as possible. Just like Olivia's colleagues, they're incented on metrics like open rates and clickthrough rates. They want to do the right thing. They want to build brands, explain product features, engage customers, and make them happy to purchase; in short, they want to pursue the same goals they learned in their marketing classes in college. But the focus is increasingly on short-term gains and conversions, not long-term relationships. And when that is your focus, you just spin the wheel faster and faster: more leads mean more email subscribers, more email subscribers create the opportunity to send more offers, and more offers generate more revenue. But as long as consumers are "targets," this can only go so far. Nobody likes to be a target. When an entitled consumer feels like a target, she rebels.

In our surveys, only 43% of consumers said that they read all the messages *from companies they like*. You can bet they're skipping lots more messages from companies they're not so fond of. Their main reason for skipping those messages, according to our survey: there are just too many of them, and they're about products and promotions that aren't relevant. To a marketer, an irrelevant promotion is just a clickthrough that didn't happen. But to the consumer, that email feels like spam.

Among the Fully Entitled consumers in our survey, one in five say they "often become annoyed with companies that don't provide the convenience, relevance, and value they expect." When you annoy an entitled consumer, a backlash isn't far behind.

Which marketers are causing these problems? Nearly all of them. When we asked an analyst who's been helping marketers make email effective for more than a decade which companies were at fault, she said, "I have so many examples. Everybody does bad email."

Nobody likes to be a target. When an entitled consumer feels like a target, she REBELS.

It's a classic problem: the tragedy of the commons. Perhaps you know the story, first popularized by biologist Garrett Hardin in the 1960s.[1] Shepherds in a town share a grazing space—the commons. Since it's a shared resource that's free to them, their tendency is to use as much of it as they can. Any individual shepherd might as well increase the size of his flock, since there's no penalty for grazing more. But as each individual makes this decision independently, the flocks grow to an unsustainable size and graze the commons down to bare dirt. The grass is gone and the whole town suffers. In the absence of rules, restraints, and costs, a shared resource becomes endangered.

The cumulative effect of all the marketing from thousands of marketers is TOTAL marketing overload.

For marketers, the commons at risk is people's attention. Consumers are distracted and besieged by ads, and our inboxes are crammed full of offers from every company we've ever bought from or visited. For the individual marketer, like the individual shepherd, there's very little downside in increasing the number and intrusiveness of the ads and messages she puts out. But the cumulative effect over thousands of marketers is total marketing overload. The overload creates numbness and increases resistance.

The problem occurs at multiple levels. Within any given company, marketers in different departments increase the frequency of messages they send. This behavior fouls the first commons: the company's overall brand impression. And across companies, there's a flood of emails trying to get at the consumer's increasingly narrow attention. This behavior fouls the second commons: the consumer's openness to marketing messages in general. Combined, these two effects create a vicious cycle: consumers tune out more and more, and marketers increase messaging frequency to try to get past their filters.

In the end, each brand suffers—and taken together, all marketing suffers. And it is only getting worse and worse. Customers expect marketers to behave better. Among the consumers we surveyed, 43% agree with the statement, "Companies are lucky to get my attention, and they should act like it." And for Fully Entitled consumers, that proportion rises to 59%.

In the rest of this chapter, we'll explore this problem in more detail. We'll look at the advertising explosion, the assault on consumers' inboxes, and the way that marketing clutter not only annoys consumers but also makes them impervious to marketing. We'll show how messaging overload undermines the one quality that helps companies retain customers: a superior customer experience. Finally, we'll explain how the only way out of this paradox for marketers is to create messages that actually engage the entitled consumer.

ADVERTISING OVERKILL

Ten years ago, Yankelovich estimated that the average person living in a city saw 5,000 marketing messages per day.[2] Since then, we've become addicted to mobile phones and social media applications that are crammed with marketing messages. The real world offers no respite: you can now read ads on turnstiles, watch ad-laden TV in the backs of taxis, read domain names on the backs and shoulders of boxers, and find coupons on the reverse side of retail receipts.

> It's not just the number of ads that creates **ANNOYANCE**, it's the inability to escape.

It's not just the number of ads that creates annoyance—it's the inability to escape.

Online advertisers have embraced the concept of retargeting. You check out a product on a website, and then ads for that product follow you relentlessly all across the web, long after you've either bought the product or given up your search for it. Jonathan Petrino, vice president at the marketing technology company Signal, calls retargeting "the Walking Dead of ads." Who couldn't relate to the experience that *NewCo* writer Lauren Hallden described in a *Medium* post called "Towards a Bra-Free Instagram Experience," which begins:[3]

> Hey Instagram, I was just wondering, does your company collect any user feedback from women? I ask because I am one, and I've noticed that my sponsored content is...well, it's a little repetitive. Kind of one-note. And I get why: somewhere, an algorithm has (correctly) identified that I do yoga, and yeah, I guess I've bought a sports bra or two in my day. And also other kinds of bras.
>
> So naturally, you'd like me to purchase more bras. Golly, there sure are lots of bras on your app! I didn't appreciate just how many barely-different strategies a company might employ to lift a pair of breasts! It's truly incredible. So thanks for opening my eyes. But here's the thing: I've started feeling like maybe you don't realize what being exposed to an endless string of half-naked, extremely thin women is doing to people like me?

But her post isn't just text. After every sentence is a picture of a bra ad that got served to her: 31 separate Instagram ads for bras and leotards and leggings, all featuring skinny women in various unlikely poses. While we, the authors, don't personally get bra ads—some algorithm, somewhere, has figured out that we don't have the necessary equipment—we can certainly relate to the sentiment.

"All of the brands are on Instagram, and they're not only there because you like them, but they're there because they target you, so there's too much of it. I started unfollowing all the brands I liked because there's just too much noise in my Instagram feed. Before I would actively follow brands, and now I've unfollowed them."

SARAH, psychologist, Germany

As TV channels have multiplied, companies can no longer realistically estimate and cap the frequency of ads. Edward Papazian, president of Media Dynamics and former research director at the agency BBDO, points out that consumers avoid commercials so much that there's no way to know which ads they are watching.[4] As a result, he says, it's "very common to see the same ad repeated on the same channel every half hour or more, often on a given day, and certain shows are vastly oversaturated with redundant ads." And don't get us started on streaming services; Hulu seems determined to show us the same irrelevant ad for Match.com five times on every show, dozens and hundreds of times a week, even after asking you whether it's relevant or not!

In the world of the entitled consumer, marketing clutter creates resentment, which creates resistance, which generally leads to some technology company coming up with a solution to block a marketing channel. According to Forrester Research, 38% of US consumers have installed an ad blocker on their browsers, and 50% actively attempt to avoid ads on websites.[5] Click rates on ads are down to 0.05% (that's one click per two thousand impressions),[6] and even those are questionable: mobile provider Retale estimates that 60% of clicks on mobile banner ads are just mistakes made by consumers tapping in the wrong spot.[7]

There's no respite on the web. Nearly every media site, from CNN to Forbes, plays video automatically when you visit. These ads work because they intrude. They follow in a long line of annoying ad trends, starting with pop-ups, pop-unders, and large ads that cover the page until you make them go away. According to a HubSpot survey, 89% of consumers agree that these sorts of intrusive ads "are really frustrating to deal with."[8] So the pattern continues: annoying ad formats create resentment, which generates technical solutions that block the ads. Sure enough, by the time you read this, Google Chrome's ad blocker will have helpfully started blocking autoplay videos on media sites.[9]

In the world of the entitled consumer, marketing clutter creates RESENTMENT, which creates resistance.

"Pop-up windows drive me nuts. Nuts!"
CHRISTINA, PR director, Germany

THE ASSAULT ON YOUR INBOX AND MOBILE DEVICES

Advertising clutter is annoying enough, but at least it's on websites and media, outside of the spaces that consumers consider their own. But some media are more sensitive—part of a consumer's more intimate, personal domain. Consumers consider their mobile devices to be much more personal than their PC, for example. Email inboxes are part of a consumer's more intimate, personal domain as well. That's why email marketing is so effective: it's gotten past the consumer's mental firewall. It's also why the more irrelevant, tone-deaf messages you send, the more consumers will tune you out.

"No one wants daily email updates [from companies]."
AMBER, nutritionist, US

We'll start with some good news on email marketing. According to Inbox Marketer, open rates on commercial emails are up, from 19% in 2011 to 29% in 2016.[10] The reason: marketers are becoming more sophisticated in how they write subject lines (including, in some cases, the recipient's name) and how they display emails on mobile devices, even as more consumers are reading these emails in spare moments on their mobile devices. Clickthrough rates vary from 1.9% to 4.3%, depending on provider and industry.

Well-meaning marketers—like the people in Olivia's auto club organization—are therefore doing what they always do with a marketing channel that works: flooding it to the point where entitled consumers will resent and evade it. The pricing of email service providers actually encourages this behavior. For example, if your email provider is salesforce.com, Oracle, or Adobe, you are charged a "cost per thousand" (CPM) for the emails you send. The more you send, the lower the CPM. So why not flood that inbox?

"As soon as the person called me from Booking.com, whatever she did on the phone, literally, within a minute, I got 200 spam emails. So I never used Booking.com again."
JESS, admin, UK

Some industry commentators encourage this behavior. For example, Dela Quist, email marketing expert and CEO of email marketing firm Alchemy Worx, told *Entrepreneur Magazine*: "What we found was, no matter what we did, more email generated more revenue. You could not stop that happening."[11] And don't bother wasting time on segmenting your email, Quist says. "It's so much easier to find one thing that entertains a million people than a million things that entertain one person each."

What Dela doesn't account for is that each undifferentiated mass email that lands in a consumer's inbox generates a tiny bit more annoyance at how that inbox is cluttered with useless crap. Dela is basically encouraging each of us to be a greedy shepherd and to just add to our flock, and the commons be damned.

We recently asked some of our friends and followers on social networks—a fairly sophisticated group—how they felt about all this marketing in their inboxes. Here's a sample of what we heard:

- "[US telecom operator] Xfinity—if you sign up with them, they barf email marketing at you and then randomly call you to market things to you. They seem to ignore any 'opt out' preferences you set."
- "Pinterest. There is no unsubscribe option to the emails notifying me of boards they just know I'm gonna love!"
- "Daily offers from the online/catalog clothing sellers. All of them. The hardest to deal with are the companies that I do want to buy from—and want to know about the specials—but not every day."
- "I found [business card vendor] Vistaprint to be so persistent in their desire to convert intent into purchase that I felt the need to resist and use a different vendor."
- "Thank goodness for the Gmail 'Promotions' [folder]—I don't even look at that crap anymore."

Consumers perceive the Promotions tab in Gmail and other similar mail clients as a way to sequester low-interest offers where they can easily avoid them. Marketers, of course, see this tab as a low-traffic part of the inbox that they're stuck in. But for entitled consumers, even the Promotions tab may not be sufficient. According to HubSpot, 54% of American consumers say that they have set up a "separate spam email [account] for commercial offers you don't want going to your main email address."[12] And 35% claim they've never bought anything based on an email from a company. When these consumers receive an unwanted commercial email, 58% of them say they then unsubscribe from the mailing list.

"I have one email account [that] I always put in for companies, and so all the spam goes there. I don't really look at it."

ANDY, teacher, Germany

"I have the same thing."

CHRISTINA, PR director, Germany

"Yeah, me too."

SARAH, psychologist, Germany

The real penalty for sending too many emails, in the end, is the constant, steady erosion of your brand that comes from overfrequent communication. Marketers who recognize this, like Olivia at the auto club, may have a hard time explaining it to their colleagues, but the effect is real.

When Ingrid Lindberg was the chief customer experience officer of the health insurer Cigna, she became concerned with the extreme volume of the messaging (mail and email) to subscribers from colleagues at her company, she finally figured out a way to make her point as dramatically as possible. She took 10,000 pieces of collateral, all of which were in active use at Cigna, stapled them together, and hung them from the ceiling of one conference room. She mounted 167 flat-screen TVs, each showing one URL that Cigna's members needed to access. "We were able to show employees that yes, they were part of the problem," she told us. As people toured through this "customer experience room," they realized that their individual message might be important to them, but to the customer, it was just one piece of a distracting and annoying blizzard of paperwork and messages.

Eventually, galvanized by this display, Cigna cut paper collateral by half, combined phone contacts into a single toll-free number, and built a single website. Cigna's stock went up tenfold even as this reduction in messaging was going on.

Your challenge is a lot like Ingrid's. Once you (and everyone else) fill up the mailboxes and inboxes of everyone who's ever been in touch with you, how will they even notice your message? And why would they even look?

CLUTTER BLINDNESS

Too many emails; too many ads; too little relevance. The net effect of this marketing assault is to attenuate the value of marketing messages. By itself, that reduction in effectiveness would be challenging enough for marketers. But even as marketing clut-

Multitasking consumers are paying less and less **ATTENTION** to the media they're consuming.

ter increases, consumers are paying less attention to the media they're consuming. Why? Because they're multitasking.

A study by the Kaiser Family Foundation found that when people under 18 use media, 29% of the time they are multitasking—listening to music, using a computer, watching TV, or playing games, for example.[13] And despite severe penalties, more people are tapping their mobile phones while driving—so much so that deaths from auto accidents rose 14% from 2014 to 2016.[14] When everyone has a mobile device within reach, they're far more likely to whip it out when commercials are airing on the TV, especially if those commercials are being repeated endlessly.

The challenge comes from limits on the "perceptual load"—the brain's theoretical capacity for receiving information. As interactive ad pioneer John Nardone, CEO of the technology startup Flashtalking, wrote in a paper on "The New Creative Paradigm":[15]

> Imagine that your brain is a bucket that can only hold so much water. When multitasking, more water might be flowing by, but the bucket can still only hold so much. This causes several adaptive effects in the brain.
>
> - **THE FILTERING EFFECT:** Also known as "inattentional blindness," when the brain's capacity to take in information is reached, it starts filtering out any information it deems to be irrelevant.

- **THE CONTROL FACTOR:** As consumers exert more control over more cluttered media (fast-forwarding DVRs, scrolling through newsfeeds, etc.), the more likely they are to "hunt" for relevant information rather than passively "gather" whatever information passes across the screen, actively blocking everything else out.

  In today's media-heavy society, people's perceptual load is often at or above capacity, whether they know it or not. Together the Filtering Effect and the Control Factor combine forces to nearly guarantee that people are ignoring irrelevant ads.

This matters to advertisers. In 2017, the Center for Research Excellence determined that consumers who were multitasking with digital devices were only half as likely to recall ads as those who weren't multitasking.[16]

Megan Burns, a customer experience expert who has studied the psychology of customer interactions, says this reaction is part of our "psychological immune system." Basically, humans have a limited capacity to process information, and when we exceed that capacity, we tune things out. And repetitive ads, irrelevant emails, intrusive text messages, and random push notifications from apps are what we stop paying attention to, regardless of how loud they are shouting.

THE CONFLICT BETWEEN MARKETING AND CUSTOMER EXPERIENCE

Really, what's the big deal? Who cares if the customers get a little bothered by the efforts of the company's marketing efforts to place ads and drive revenue with emails? If a few customers get annoyed and a few more spend money, where's the harm?

The answer can be measured in customer experience.

What do we mean by customer experience? In their book *Outside In: The Power of Putting Customers at the Center of Your Business*, Harley Manning and Kerry Bodine define it this way: "Customer experience is how your customers perceive their interaction with your company."[17] (We go into more detail about customer experience in chapter 6.)

This is not some squishy, feel-good concept. You can measure it through analytical systems that measure retention and repeat sales, surveys based on concepts like Net Promoter Score, analyses of social media posts and sentiment, transcripts from contact and call centers, online feedback tools, and similar business metrics.

Does customer experience matter?

Customer experience leaders see five times the **REVENUE GROWTH** of laggards, on average.

There's a lot of evidence that it does. In *Outside In*, the authors demonstrate how scores on the Forrester Research Customer Experience Index correlate strongly with customers' willingness to consider additional purchases from the company and their likelihood to recommend the company to friends and colleagues. When Watermark Consulting analyzed the eight-year stock performance of companies evaluated by Forrester in 2015, customer experience leaders showed a cumulative return of 108%, compared to a return of 28% for customer experience laggards (and 72% for the S&P 500).[18]

In fact, according to Forrester, customer experience leaders see, on average, over five times the revenue growth of CX laggards.[19]

Marketing need not be the ENEMY of a good customer experience.

Marketing is not necessarily the enemy of a good customer experience, but unless it is carefully managed, it can be. When marketers become too focused on the bottom-of-funnel metrics, they can go off course. As Gartner customer experience analyst Augie Ray has written, marketers "must stop overvaluing what is easy to measure and recognize that what's hard to measure is frequently more powerful...[E]asy measures are important but not predictive of future success, such as clicks and conversions."[20]

When there is too much irrelevant messaging, customers penalize the brand for a poor experience. Customer experience expert Megan Burns describes how overzealous marketing pushed some customers of a large nonprofit organization to their breaking point. The group sent dozens of solicitations to potential donors, in part because data showed that more messages led to more donations short term. What the data didn't show, though, was the resentment brewing; donors started to call the organization and say, "I donated to you once but won't do so again because all of this mail you're sending me feels like harassment." Those donors, who may still support the organization's cause, had been driven away, and it was too late to get them back.

There is a natural tension here. It is not only a tension between marketing and customer experience. It is a tension between the short-term need to close business and the long-term goal of maintaining the brand and customer relationships. It is a tension between the need for scale to make marketing efficient and the need for intimacy to make customers feel valued.

WE CAN DO BETTER

Marketers, at their core, want to do the right thing. They want to make customers aware of products or services that will make them happier. They want to build brands. The challenge has been to deliver on that promise in an efficient way. But too many are unable to act on the knowledge they have.

Case in point: I (Dave) was recently traveling and had exactly this thought. I took an Uber to the airport in Florida. I landed in Boston and took two separate Ubers there. Then I flew to L.A. and took an Uber to a suburb there.

Meanwhile, in my inbox, I received email promotions for UberEats in New York and San Francisco—two cities where I had not actually touched down on this trip. Uber, a company whose business model is centered on knowing your location, knew exactly where I was. Why not advertise UberEats in L.A.?

Companies have the data they need to do marketing better.

Their apps know where we are.

Their customer systems know what we've bought.

Their messaging systems, properly configured, know what we've clicked on and responded to in the past.

Why can't they give us what we're most likely to want?

That's the topic of the next chapter.

THE CONSUMER-FIRST MARKETER'S TO-DO LIST

These are your to-dos to recognize the impact of marketing overload:

- ☐ Identify all the sources within your organization of messages sent to customers, including different departments, product lines, and service and marketing organizations.
- ☐ Find ways to measure messaging volume at the customer level, and look for signs of overload.
- ☐ Find creative ways to bring the messaging overload to light, and make managers across the organization aware of it.
- ☐ Assess the cost to your brand of retargeting and ad repetition; what's the cost of a consumer shutting you out?
- ☐ Maintain email marketing effectiveness by increasing relevance and decreasing frequency.

WE NEED TO IMPROVE SERVICE
WE CAN'T AFFORD IT
WE'RE INVESTING EVERYTHING INTO PROMOTIONS
CONSUMERS ONLY BUY FROM US IF WE GIVE IT AWAY
WHY WON'T CONSUMERS PAY FULL PRICE?
BECAUSE OUR SERVICE IS SO BAD
TOM FISH BURNE
© marketoonist.com

Chapter 3

CONSUMER-FIRST MARKETING

Jennifer Stamper cares about storage.

More accurately, she cares about people who need to store things. Jennifer is the interactive marketing manager for Extra Space Storage, the second-largest operator of self-storage facilities in America. She started there as an intern, fell in love with marketing, took over the company's email program, and now manages all contacts with the company's 900,000 customers.

If you're like most storage space customers, you don't like to think much about storage. It's one of those get-it-and-forget-it kind of relationships for people moving out, moving up, moving into a new place, or moving in with relatives. That means every customer communication from Extra Space needs to help, or you'll probably tune it out. And storage is a boring product: three concrete walls and a garage door. Nobody wants to hear about that.

Jennifer takes that as a challenge. "We pride ourselves on our innovation," she told us, "and our ability to create a contextual relationship around a product that they might not be very excited about."

The key to that relationship is knowledge. Extra Space knows when you're moving. The company knows how far in advance you've made the reservation for storage space. It knows where you live and how big a space you're renting. And it knows whether you're a typical consumer storing your personal stuff or a business customer, like a shop owner storing inventory or a pharmaceutical rep with a climate-controlled space for supplies.

That may not seem like much, but it's just enough to send exactly the right message at the right moment.

If you're a renter in Miami who reserved a unit at least 14 days in advance, Jennifer's email system infers that you're a planner and might send you information about security, pest control, insurance, and leases. And if the forecast for your moving day calls for rain, you'll get tips for moving in bad weather and how to protect your electronics.

If you're a homeowner moving to Dallas, you'll get tips on the local restaurants that can keep you fed as you move your stuff.

If you're a pharma rep in Boise, you're probably a high-value customer who's going to get an email about efficient ways to organize in a small space, including pictures of customers just like you with their neatly set-up storage spaces.

All of this matters because of the Extra Space business model. Reservations are free and come with no obligation. Customers only have to pay if they show up and use the space. So Jennifer and her marketing colleagues really want you to follow through on your reservation.

Since Jennifer put in place a solution for personalized email, the company's conversion rate attributable to email (the percentage of contacts who actually end up renting) is up by 50%. And because people on the move are mobile, Extra Space's mobile-friendly emails and website have boosted rentals via mobile devices by 23%, without any corresponding decrease in rentals from computer screens.

The true test of the system came in 2017, when monster hurricanes in Houston, Texas, and all across Florida and Puerto Rico slammed the company's customers and buildings. Before the heavy weather hit, Extra Space sent carefully localized communications to customers about when the storage facilities would be open ahead of the storms and when they'd be locked down. Afterward, things got even more challenging. For example, in one Houston location, some storage buildings were underwater but others were fine, while in Florida, Hurricane Irma had ripped the roof off a block of storage units in one location. Extra Space sent carefully timed, personalized messages to the customers affected by these misfortunes—and *only* the affected customers. That works a lot better than sending everyone with a unit in Florida a message like, "Warning, some units have been damaged," needlessly upsetting customers already reeling from a natural disaster.

Jennifer modestly characterized the response from customers as "a lot of really good feedback." She's still analyzing data from these locations and from customers affected by wildfires in California. The company will fold all of what it learns into even more personal and useful messages. Because while people don't spend a lot of time thinking about their storage, they're grateful when they get the right message at the right moment, based on who they are and everything happening around them.

YOU'VE GOT A FRIEND

Philosophically, the way Extra Space Storage does digital marketing is attractive. That's because the company behaves like a friend instead of a loudmouthed boor.

When you invite a loudmouthed boor to your house, he won't shut up. He talks about what's important to him. He has no idea what's going on in your life, and he doesn't seem to care. He makes generalizations about you based on your age or where you live or shop, then acts on those generalizations without checking whether they even apply to you. And once he thinks he knows you, he'll text you, email you, show up on your Facebook feed, and follow you all around town.

Most marketers, no matter how well intentioned, tend to come off like that loudmouthed boor, emailing repeated, generalized messages at will and popping up ads that follow you all across the web and social media. This isn't because marketers are evil; it's because they use tools that make it easy to bug you—and because it's cheap and effective in the short term. It's also because of common monthly or quarterly marketing incentives and goals focused around closing business. As we described in the previous chapter, the loudmouthed-boor approach delivers a certain amount of quick conversions, even if in the long term it damages your brand.

> **To be an effective consumer-first marketer, BEHAVE like a friend, not a loudmouthed boor.**

But Jennifer and Extra Space aren't behaving like loudmouthed boors. They're behaving like a friend. They think about what's going on in your life and how they can help you. If it's going to rain on the day they know you'll be moving, they'll remind you how to keep your stuff covered up. If you're new in town, they'll tell you where to get great takeout on moving day. If they won't be available when you need them because, say, a hurricane is coming, they'll let you know when they *will* be available. And if something happened to your belongings while in their care, they'll let you know—*but if something didn't, they won't worry you with a false alarm.*

A friend understands who you are and what's important to you.

A marketer who behaves like a friend UNDERSTANDS who you are and what's important to you.

A friend watches how you react to what she says, then changes how she communicates. If you like texting, she'll text you; if you'd rather get an email, she'll email you.

A friend takes everything she knows about you—where you live, what you did together in the past, whether you like to be spontaneous or plan in advance, whether you like to fit in with the crowd or stand out, your likes and dislikes, even what time it is—and gives you whatever you need most at the moment you need it.

Here's the thing about friendships: The friends who listen and give you what you need are valuable. You tend to keep them around a long time, because the relationship benefits both sides.

> *"On Instagram, I tend to follow brands and cool accounts, but when they put out stuff I don't like, I unfollow them right away."*
>
> **RAGNA,** web producer, Sweden

Of course, in business, companies can't credibly say they are the consumer's friend (see sidebar). They are commercial organizations trying to make money. But if they can learn to treat their customers right, they'll earn loyalty. And in the age of the entitled consumer, loyalty is a very valuable commodity.

Not all friendships are created equal

We've talked about the things a friend would do, as opposed to a loudmouthed boor. But people have all sorts of friends. There are the ones who feed your cat when you're traveling, the ones who comfort you when you're depressed, and the ones you like to play golf with.

In the same way, customer relationships have a lot of variety as well. Business professor Susan Fournier[1] introduced the notion of consumer-brand relationships to marketing in the late 1990s, and she and her colleagues Jill Avery and John Wittenbraker have worked hard to help managers measure the portfolio of relationships consumers form with their brands. Their perspective, based on extensive survey research on more than 200 brands in 11 industries and eight countries, is that most customer-relationship management (CRM) systems do not address the diversity of those relationships, which causes problems because sensitivity to relationship types and their different rules for engagement is the key to effective relationship management. As they write, "Despite the 'R' in CRM and the $11 billion spent on CRM software annually, many companies don't understand customer relationships at all. They lack relational intelligence—that is, they aren't aware of the variety of relationships customers can have with a firm and don't know how to reinforce or change those connections."[2]

These researchers have identified and validated 29 different types of consumer-brand relationships. For example, a "basic exchange" relationship customer is just looking for a decent product at a fair price. In a "fling," the consumer uses the product to exper-

iment with a new identity or generate intense emotional rewards. Consumers with "secret affairs" keep their consumption hidden from others—for example, people who buy Cheetos hide them in their cars and work hard to erase the orange dust on their fingers that would reveal their affair with the brand. A customer in a "master-slave" relationship with a brand wants the company to do her bidding to intensify feelings of self-worth—for example, an American Airlines "Concierge Key" customer who expects the airline to hold aside upgrades and delay connecting flights if her incoming plane is late.

Fournier highlights the iconic American motorcycle manufacturer Harley-Davidson as an example of a brand relationship that is more like a friendship. "Friends are there when you need them," she told us. Harley-Davidson "never sells you info, violates your privacy, or takes advantage of you." When the company considered raising fees for membership in its Harley Owners Group (HOG) customer community, it quickly rejected the ideas, because a friend would never take advantage that way.

We find this research instructive. As you build your consumer-first marketing program, consider the different types of customers you have and the types of relationships they have or will prefer (see figure 6). This type of thinking is why customer-first marketing is different for Extra Space Storage compared to Harley-Davidson and, even within a brand, may be different depending on the line of business or whether the customer is a new buyer, a repeat buyer, or a frequently returning customer.

Figure 6: The variety of customer relationships

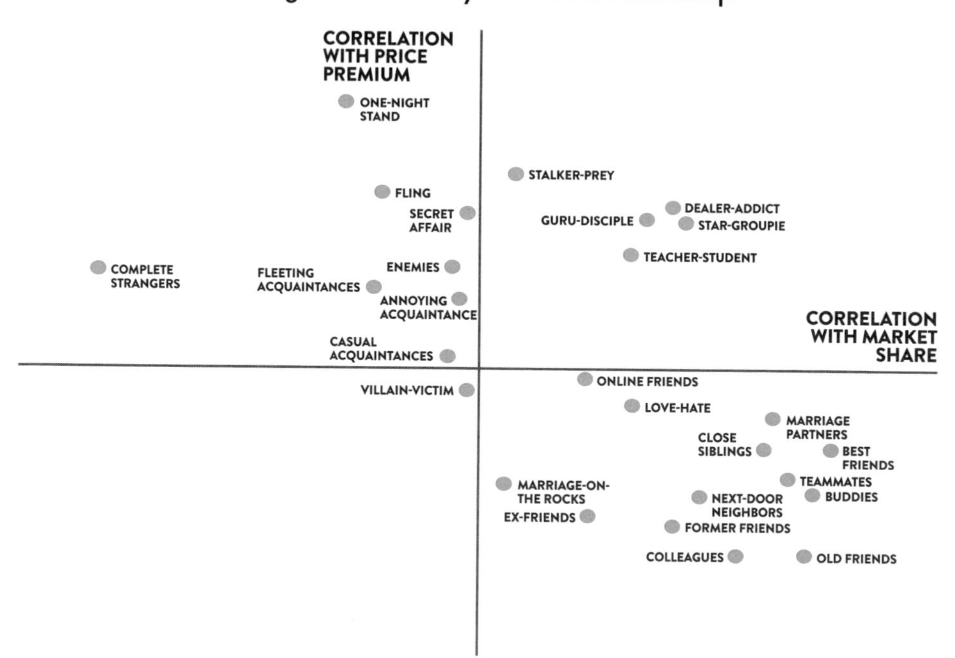

Source: "Unlock the Mysteries of Your Customer Relationships," by Jill Avery, Susan Fournier, and John Wittenbraker, July–August 2014, Harvard Business Review. Used by permission.

In the rest of this chapter, we'll describe consumer-first marketing, a philosophy that treats customers more as a friend would instead of treating them the way a loudmouthed boor would. We'll show you how your current marketer-first efforts will increasingly fall short. We'll explain why now is the moment when this new kind of marketing is not just possible but necessary. And then we'll show you what happens when marketers start doing it.

WHAT CONSUMER-FIRST MARKETING IS, AND WHAT IT ISN'T

A small but growing number of organizations have figured out what Jennifer Stamper and Extra Space Storage know: that marketing should start not with the marketer but with the consumer. We call their philosophy "consumer-first marketing." We define it this way:

> *Consumer-first marketing inverts the traditional approach to marketing. Instead of starting with the product or communications channel, this strategy focuses first on consumers to identify opportunities for filling an unmet need, entertaining, or solving a pressing problem.*

This is not an entirely new vision. In fact, 25 years ago, Don Peppers and Martha Rogers described some of these elements in their groundbreaking book *The One to One Future*. But they were ahead of their time, because the future that they imagined was, when they imagined it, out of reach and impossible to deliver efficiently (see sidebar).

Many marketers found the one-to-one marketing vision compelling. But to put it into practice, the best they could do was to identify large groups—"cohorts," such as women aged 35-54—and then turn those groups into marketing targets. Don Peppers and Martha Rogers' one-to-one future remained a visionary idea, impossible to realize in practice, because there was no practical way to identify what a particular consumer wanted in a particular moment. That's changed now. One-to-one marketing is now possible and is becoming more practical every day.

Don Peppers' one-to-one vision comes to life

In their 1993 book The One to One Future, *Don Peppers and Martha Rogers imagined a new way of marketing. As they wrote at the time:*

> *Most businesses follow time-honored mass-marketing rules of pitching their products to the greatest number of people. However, selling more goods to fewer people is not only more efficient but more profitable...*The One to One Future *is a radically innovative business paradigm focusing on the share of customer—one customer at a time—rather than just the share of market.*

They describe a philosophy in which companies don't just shout messages at customers but instead pursue relationships to build repeat business, spending more on retention and less on customer acquisition. Their vision of the future of marketing included focusing on managing customers over managing products, engaging in dialogue with customers to learn more about their needs, and protecting privacy as a differentiating tactic.

The One to One Future *describes this shift as a "discontinuity" in the market. And indeed, many of the changes that the authors predicted two decades ago have come to pass. Take, for example, today's much greater focus on customer segmentation and targeting. Companies have widely adopted customer relationship management (CRM) systems that allow them to understand and address individual customers' service needs and history in their contact centers. A few pioneering marketers have followed, and business-to-business marketers selling six- and seven-figure relationships still use the Peppers and Rogers playbook.*

But, as Don confirmed when we interviewed him, most market-

ers still treat their customers as a mass market, bombarding them with undifferentiated messages. Today's reality is very far from the one-to-one future painted in the book, despite the acclaim it has enjoyed in 25 years since its publication.

Part of the problem stems from companies' focus on the short term. As Don explains, "You can spend a lot of time crafting loyalty and good feeling, but it only pays off later." This is a challenge because it doesn't show up on the balance sheet. "The vast majority of companies aren't doing one-to-one marketing because they have the wrong metrics in place," he says. "We run on a nineteenth-century accounting system that doesn't account for the customers having any value whatsoever. Companies are so maniacally focused on short-term reporting of earnings and sales; they are unable to reconcile that with the investment required to create long-term value for customers. I can't tell you how stupid accounting programs are in Western economies."

The other problem has been a lack of technology that could actually implement the one-to-one vision for marketers. But now that technology exists, and companies like Amazon are pointing the way to the future that Don saw 25 years ago. "For my money, Amazon is the world's most authentically customer-oriented company," Don says. "It's an extremely frictionless way to buy. Jeff Bezos is very tightly focused on the value that his customer franchise represents. Because of the share of each customer's trust that Amazon enjoys, expectations are rising; my expectations of the next company I do business with has gone up." Like us, Don has observed the transference of entitlement from companies like Amazon to every other company on the planet, a phenomenon we will be discussing in more detail in chapter 6.

Don Peppers also agrees with our concept that companies must treat customer relationships more as friendships than as mar-

keting targets. "There is a new standard," he told us. "A customer wants to be treated the way a friend would treat a friend. That's how technology would permit a company to behave in the future. You can use algorithms and automation to do that; customers are beginning to expect it."

There's a critical role for people in Don's vision as well—they provide the human touch rather than just building the campaigns and assaulting consumers with them. "That's the future," he says, "fusing employees' human judgment, wisdom, creativity, and empathy into the algorithms, to develop better, more effective relationships with customers."

Take note: Don sees marketers at the forefront of this charge. "Marketers are the proselytizers for this process," he says. "It's an uphill battle, but they have a big role to play, pitching this case internally."

Unfortunately, none of us marketers were ever trained to think about marketing in a personalized way. Instead, we start with our own problems and familiar methods—methods that are becoming increasingly ineffective. This is marketer-first marketing—it treats consumers as a target, and they know it. Marketer-first marketing includes three subcategories: product-first marketing, channel-first marketing, and cohort-first marketing. All three have problems.

Product-first marketing meets your needs but not the consumer's

Suppose you have 500,000 pairs of cargo pants to sell. If that's what's in stock, you send out a marketing message about cargo pants. But tastes change. If nobody's wearing cargo pants right now, you're selling what people don't want. You're the loudmouthed boor again.

This kind of thing happens all the time. For example, at one large North American bank, we heard about customers in the midst of negotiating home equity loans receiving pitches for car loans. From the marketer's perspective, this makes a strange kind of sense—why not send car loan solicitations to everybody and see who bites? But to the consumer about to take the major step of collecting the paperwork and applying for a home equity loan, perhaps with the help of a loan officer at the bank, it just feels like harassment. The consumer doesn't know or care that there are different business units inside the bank, each with their own metrics, that want to convert them into a customer of their business unit. Whatever trust the loan officer created is squandered, and the customer becomes resentful. The bank's brand image changes in the mind of the consumers who got bugged to get a car loan, and they begin to perceive the bank not as a friend but as a loudmouthed boor.

One-to-one marketing is now possible and is becoming more **PRACTICAL** every day.

Do people expect more of brands? Sure they do. In our survey of European and American consumers, 70% of consumers agreed with the statement, "When a company interacts with me, it's important that they understand my current situation and not just try to sell me their product." Among Fully Entitled consumers, 95% agree that selling without understanding your current situation is a problem and 45% agree that, "It's shocking how bad companies are at knowing who I am or understanding my needs." If you're intent on reaching Fully Entitled consumers, you'll have do better than product-first marketing.

The customer has NO INTEREST in your internal organizational dynamics.

Channel-first marketing creates a disjointed experience

Even as they push products, most marketers have another challenge: disjointed channels. This tends to happen when your team is organized around channels: stores or branches, websites, mobile apps, emails, text messages, call centers, and so on. Each of these marketing groups pursues its own strategy and has its own goals to achieve. But the customer has no interest in your internal organizational dynamics—to her, it's just a tone-deaf set of messages that don't seem to recognize that they're targeted at a single consumer.

Consumers are noticing. According to a survey of 7,000 consumers by salesforce.com, 81% expect companies to provide the same level of service every time they interact with a brand, and 75% expect a consistent experience regardless of what channel they're coming in from.[3]

Even so, most marketers are still using channel-specific tools to manage their campaigns. When Econsultancy surveyed almost 2,000 digital marketers in 2015, it found that half of them had separate, nonconnected technologies managing data for different channels.[4] Only 17% were fully capable of analyzing their customers' journeys, and only one-quarter had the tools to manage campaigns across channels.

Again, consumers don't want mixed-up messages across channels. In our own survey, 76% of European and North American consumers (and 95% of Fully Entitled consumers) agreed with the statement, "When I sign up for something, I expect to control how and when the company contacts me (e.g., email, text messages, phone calls, mobile...)." Your customers want to control how you use marketing channels. Are you listening?

Cohort-first marketing lumps unlike people together

> Consumers know you use cohorts, and they're **DISGUSTED** by it.

Some companies feel they've mastered how to market in a more targeted way. Rather than sending the same message to all their customers in all their channels, they divide people up into cohorts, mostly by age, income, or location. They recognize that Millennials want something different from Generation Xers, who want something different from Baby Boomers.

This approach is only marginally better than the others, because generations are not monolithic blocs in which everyone is similar.

For example, while it seems like marketers are finally ready to embrace the proposition that "Millennials are different," they haven't recognized that, actually, "Each Millennial is different"—that is, they don't all react in the same way. For example, many Millennials ridiculed presidential candidate Hillary Clinton when she tweeted, "How does your student loan debt make you feel? Tell us in three emojis or less." As Albizu Garcia, CEO of collaboration tools company Gain, explains, "This large demographic that would struggle to remember a time before the internet is jaded to old-school advertising that puts forth any insincerity or misrepresentation to increase sales. But the overarching commonalities in the generation pretty much stop there."[5]

Most consumers know you use cohorts, and they're disgusted by it. In our survey of American and European consumers, 74% agreed that "I expect companies to treat me as an individual, not as a member of some segment like 'Millennials' or 'suburban mothers.'" It's not just Millennials; nobody likes to be treated as one member of a huge anonymous group (see sidebar).

Even if you break down generational groups into smaller subgroups, like soccer moms or urban elites, you won't hit the mark squarely. Not only is everyone different, but their needs vary from moment to moment. You need a level of precision that goes way beyond personas and cohorts. You need the familiarity that only a friend would have. You need consumer-first marketing.

Business-to-business marketers have unlocked some of these principles already

Business-to-business marketers often sell big-ticket items. As a result, they can't afford to have a messaging system that's not aware of what's going on with prospective customers. If your sales rep is closing a $250,000 sale for a software system or an insurance policy, an errant email could derail the whole deal.

As a result, B2B marketers often put rules in place—for example, suspending email marketing when there's an active negotiation above a certain price point. They think about how they interact with the customer in different circumstances—and in the case of B2B firms, different roles—and what the right message is to send based on the sale cycle and the recipient's role.

They've learned what consumer marketers ought to know by now: The customer's context makes all the difference when that customer receives a marketing message.

WHY NOW IS THE MOMENT FOR CONSUMER-FIRST MARKETING

Marketers are skeptical when we start describing consumer-first marketing. We can't blame them. In the past ten years, they have been told that social media, mobile apps, programmatic advertising, and omnichannel commerce will be their salvation.

They've carefully and skeptically evaluated each pronouncement and slowly and prudently absorbed these techniques into their repertoire. Why should marketing be any different now?

There are two main reasons. First, the amount of data that you can now bring to bear to improve your customer's experience is staggering. And second, consumers are not just ready, but expectant that you will.

More data means more opportunity for relevant messages

Consider for a moment what you know about your customer.

If you are a bank, you know not just how much money that customer has but how her balances vary day by day, week by week, and month by month. If she has a credit card, you know what she's spending money on and where. If she has teenage children, you probably know about their accounts as well. You may know about her investments and the value of her house. Shouldn't it be possible to anticipate what she might want to do with her money on a day-to-day basis?

If you are an airline, you know how often your customer travels with you, on which days of the week, and to where. If she's using your points program, you may know more about when and why she rents cars and stays in hotels—or doesn't. Shouldn't it be possible to anticipate her next set of travel needs?

If you are a retailer, you know how often your customer shops with you, what kinds of things she buys, what she returns, and whether she has visited your website, used your mobile app, or responded to your emails. Shouldn't it be possible to anticipate what sorts of products she might be thinking about next?

Consumers **EXPECT** you to use the data you have about them.

Consumer-first marketers know more than just the mass of information that their companies are gathering about their consumers. They also know what's happening in the real world. They know the weather forecast. They know the traffic conditions. They know what the stock market did today. These data feeds are easily accessible. Combined with the data the company has, they are what make it possible for an organization to do what Extra Space Storage did—to anticipate that a rainstorm in Kansas City next Tuesday might make a big difference in the life of a customer and to prepare that customer with appropriate information.

Here's a basic example. I (Josh) was recently vacationing in Palm Springs, California. On the day that I was scheduled to fly back to Boston, I picked up my phone and opened the American Airlines app. Because it knew I was flying that day, the app popped up the record for the flight home. But it also identified where I was relative to the airport and the amount of traffic between the two locations. A message just below the flight record indicated that it would take 27 minutes to drive to the airport. That's a pretty pertinent piece of information, delivered right at the moment it was needed. I was impressed (and left for the airport right on time).

IDC predicts that there will be 44 trillion gigabytes in the digital universe in 2020—up nearly ten times from 2013.[6] They also estimate that only 10% of it is ever analyzed or used by companies. The data exists; consumers are creating more every day. The question is: can you take advantage of it? (We delve deeper into that question in the next chapter.)

More entitled consumers mean higher expectations for how you will use that data

If data fuels your consumer-first marketing strategy, the reason you must use it is that consumers, increasingly, expect you to.

Technology giants have set the standard here. Amazon suggests purchases based on an extensive history of products you've bought in the past. Former Facebook executive Sam Lessin told Robert Scoble and Shel Israel, the authors of the book *Age of Context*, that the social network "wants to build a system that anticipates your needs and can offer you help at the moment you want it, and then not bother you with anything once you have made a decision."[7] Google's personal assistant for Android assembles information from your schedule with local conditions like weather and traffic and alerts you to what's coming up in your day and whether you'll be able to get to it.

Once you get used to that level of attention and intelligence, you begin to expect it from every company you deal with. According to a survey of 1,500 consumers by Michael Brenner, CEO of Marketing Insider Group, 88% of consumers say that personally relevant content improves how they feel about a brand, and 78% say it increases their purchase intent for a brand's products and services.[8] Our own surveys reinforce this, showing that the more entitled a consumer feels, the more likely she is to have increased service expectations based on the data that a company collects.

> *"I'm looking for streamlined efficiency. I want a company that is very efficient, that learns who I am in two minutes."*
>
> **ABITHIA,** graduate student, US

It's not just what they want that matters here—it's what they do when they don't get it. According to salesforce.com, 65% of consumers are likely to switch brands if a company doesn't make an effort to personalize communications to them.[9] Switching has costs, because it is so much more expensive to acquire a customer than to retain one.

For one thing, as Angela Sanfilippo of customer data platform AgileOne estimates, a company typically loses 60% of a customer's future lifetime value when that customer unsubscribes.[10] And Bain's Fred Riechheld, the inventor of the Net Promoter Score, estimates that in financial services, a 5% increase in customer retention produces more than a 25% increase in profit because of the value of return customers.[11]

"When I log in to Tesco to order shopping online and they've got my favorites, my 'last list'—that just makes my life so much easier."

KAREN, financial counselor, UK

A personalized approach gets you the attention you need. In a 2013 survey by Harris Interactive, 82% people said they were willing to accept more emails *as long as the new correspondence had taken into account past shopping habits.*[12]

CONSUMER-FIRST MARKETING IS HARD—BUT GETTING STARTED WITH IT ISN'T

Consumer-first marketing is a philosophy that says you'll reach out to people based on what you know about them personally and their situation, not just what you happened to need to sell at the moment. And while it's hard to fully embrace, it's not that hard to get started down this path. Let's look at some brands that did that.

One great example is the French cosmetics company, Etat Pur, a company whose tag line is *À chaque peau sa solution* ("for each skin, its own solution"). "We don't just sell products," Maelle Ricard, who was in charge of relationship marketing for the company, told us. "You have to go further in the way you sell the products, the relationship, so they continue to buy your products."

This is not just lip service. Etat Pur's website can query the consumer about everything that affects her skin: how dry or oily it is, the amount of sun she gets, how much she sleeps, whether she smokes, and what particular problems are bothering her, like blemishes or wrinkles. If you call the company, a counselor asks questions about similar elements of the consumer's particular skin-care needs. And the richest source of information, of course, is her purchase history, which tells Etat Pur which products appeal to that particular customer.

Before it can use this knowledge, Etat Pur must analyze what it knows about skin care. This analysis comes from the expertise of its scientific staff and beauty counselors and from looking at which of its many products are typically bought together. The result is that every outbound communication reflects what that particular, individual consumer might be most interested in at the moment. If you are 60, you won't get a pitch for cream that clears up blemishes, and if you're 20, you won't get wrinkle cream; instead, you'll get offers for products that match your particular skin type and situation, based on whether you're a smoker, or pregnant, or like to spend time in the sun. These marketing messages are enhanced with photos that match the lifestyle of the customer. Etat Pur's metrics include repurchases, frequency of buying, satisfaction measures, time spent on site, and email open rates. Based on those measures, the company is succeeding.

> *"I like that when I purchase the same thing on a website, like my makeup, I will just go back in and it's there [and ready for me]."*
>
> **JESS,** admin, UK

Personalized communication has also boosted the marketing metrics at InterContinental Hotel Group, which sends individualized communications to each customer based on location, hotel preference, travel history, loyalty level, travel preferences, website searches, and other information. Real-time weather information improves the relevance of the emails; if a customer goes back to an email to get information for an upcoming stay, the weather forecast automatically refreshes with up-to-date information. Result: the open rate for IHG emails is an impressive 68%.

Some consumer-first marketing ideas are incredibly simple. For example, if you buy a house from Redfin, a real estate company, you'll receive a note the first time there's a significant snowfall at the location of your new home.[13] Redfin reminds you to send a picture of your snow-covered home and share it on social media. It might be years after you bought the house, but you'll associate warm feelings with Redfin, which might put you in the mood to call the Redfin real estate agency again when it's time to sell the house and buy a new one.

These simple examples are the beginning of a major shift. As we'll describe in the next chapter, Boston Consulting Group has estimated that $800 billion in revenue will shift to companies that pursue personalized marketing and service and away from those that don't.

If you think you can't do consumer-first marketing yet, consider these examples. Then ask yourself if you can at least get started down the path of being more of a friend—and less of a loudmouthed boor—to your customer base.

SOPHIA'S STORY: A CONSUMER-FIRST MARKETING SCENARIO

Instead of telling you about consumer-first marketing, we'll show you. Here's a story about one consumer's experience with a retailer that uses consumer-first marketing techniques. Many of the elements of this scenario are realistic, using technologies that are available today. The challenge is putting it all together. As we relate this story, we'll point out the elements of consumer-first marketing and how they relate to the chapters coming up in this book.

This is the story of Sophia Green, a young woman in Brooklyn, New York, as she and Hailey's, a clothing and accessories retailer, get to know each other.

Sophia loves yoga. She first discovers Hailey's when a Google search for "cool yoga leggings" leads her to a product page on the Hailey's website. Hailey's is a consumer-first marketer. At the foundation of this philosophy is a focus on getting to know the customer. So, as Sophia browses through the leggings on the Hailey's site, a window pops up offering her a 10% discount for signing up on the site with her Facebook account and email. Sophia gets a deal—and Hailey's begins to learn who Sophia is, allowing it to establish a more fruitful relationship.

Data is central to any consumer-first marketing strategy. See chapter 4.

Thanks to Facebook, Hailey's knows Sophia lives in Brooklyn, is 28 years old, has a boyfriend, and likes yoga, traveling, and rock music. She chooses to give Hailey's permission to know her location. She's no longer a generic consumer. Hailey's will use this information carefully to bring her more of what she's actually likely to be looking for.

Hailey's applies analytics to the growing knowledge it's gaining about its new customer. It identifies other women whose profiles are similar to Sophia's and the knowledge the company has gained about what those women respond to. As a result, any subsequent messages to Sophia will be carefully calibrated to what Hailey's knows about her.

One day, as Sophia stops by a coffee shop on the way to work, Hailey's pushes a message to her phone indicating that there's a store nearby with a brand-new shipment of spring clothing. She taps "maybe later." Hailey's learns from this. The company now knows that on weekdays, she's not as likely to respond to messages sent in the morning.

A few days later, when Sophia is at work, she opens an email from Hailey's. It features pictures of yoga gear and rock-and-roll T-shirts, matched up to the interests that Hailey's knows Sophia has. The email isn't static, either: it configures itself dynamically when Sophia opens it. And as a result, it can show her a map of the nearest store, right in the email. She browses the gear but doesn't buy.

That weekend, after yoga class, Sophia is checking Instagram on her phone. Hailey's displays an ad showing the shirt she had browsed—but didn't buy—just a few days earlier.

She visits the Hailey's site again the following day. Her version of the site is not the same as it is for everyone else. The site now features yoga gear and the rock-and-roll T-shirt, including how many are in stock at the store nearest her.

Relevance is a key pillar of consumer-first marketing. See chapter 7.

As the months go by and Sophia buys more products, Hailey's develops a much more complete picture of her. This means that when a retargeting ad appears as she's viewing the *New York Times*, it's not for the product she's already bought; it features a warm sweatshirt in a similar style, well suited to both her previous choices and the chill in the air as New York enters the fall. She checks out the sweatshirt but doesn't buy it. A little later, she gets a Facebook messenger message about it. That message appears at a specific time—lunchtime on a weekday—and in a specific channel—Facebook messenger—because Hailey's artificial intelligence engine predicts that's when she's most open to messages from them. This tips her over into buying, so she reserves the item to pick up in the store.

When she arrives at the store and gives her name to pick up the product, the store associate can immediately identify her and see her history on his iPad. As the associate is getting the sweatshirt, he suggests a red dress that the iPad indicates Sophia would be open to buying, based on her history. Sophia goes into the dressing room and tries on the dress, which she really likes.

The consumer wants you to use your knowledge about her in every channel. See chapter 5.

The mirror in the dressing has an interactive display. It suggests a handbag to match the dress. It's perfectly suited to her style, based on all that Hailey's knows about her. She leaves the dressing room and tells the store associate she'd like the dress and the handbag as well.

Deliver reciprocal value to the consumer in every interaction. See chapter 6.

The handbag is not in stock, so the store associate places an order for her. It only takes one touch on his iPad, since all her information—including her payment details—is stored with Hailey's.

Now the handbag is on its way. Hailey's sends Sophia a confirmation email with a link to track its progress; two days later, in the morning, a text message tells her the handbag will be delivered between 1:00 and 3:00 p.m. Sure enough, the package arrives. But sadly, the handbag has a scratch on it.

Now Sophia calls Hailey's customer service on her mobile phone. Thanks to her phone number, as soon as he answers the phone, the telephone rep sees her history. He knows two important things: that she just had a handbag delivered and that she's a valuable repeat customer. So when she asks for help, he offers to air-express a replacement bag to her. His system automatically flags her account as in the middle of a problem-resolution process. As a result, Hailey's stops sending her any marketing messages—no texts, no Facebook messages, and no emails—until the new bag arrives.

Respect for the consumer is central to building relationships. See chapter 8.

Everything that Hailey's knows about Sophia makes the experience better. Hailey's knows what she likes, what she reads, where she shops, and when she responds to messages. It doesn't bombard her with noise about generic sales or target her with ads for things she's already bought. Sophia likes shopping where she's treated like a friend.

THE CONSUMER-FIRST MARKETING FRAMEWORK

Sophia's scenario is right around the corner. Companies like Indochino, which we describe in chapter 10, are implementing elements of this type of marketing already. The technology to deliver consumer-first marketing exists now. And once companies start deploying it intelligently, their competitors that are still doing marketer-first marketing will look increasingly stodgy and boorish. They'll only be able to compete on price. And that's a very dangerous position to compete from.

> *"I'm comfortable with paying more if I become comfortable that a company is treating me right."*
>
> **KEISHA,** customer service rep, US

In the rest of this book, we'll describe how you can get moving with consumer-first marketing. By observing successful marketers like Extra Space Storage that are already embracing this philosophy, we've identified the key elements of consumer-first marketing framework that help create and strengthen consumer relationship (see figure 7).

At the center of consumer-first marketing are two interconnected elements: an approach to gathering the broadest possible collection of useful data, as we describe in chapter 4, and an omnichannel mechanism for connecting with consumers across all channels—web, email, ads, apps, and in real-world interactions—in a coordinated way, which we cover in chapter 5.

Once those elements are in place, marketers need a consumer-first strategy that builds on them. That strategy includes three

Figure 7: The consumer-first marketing framework

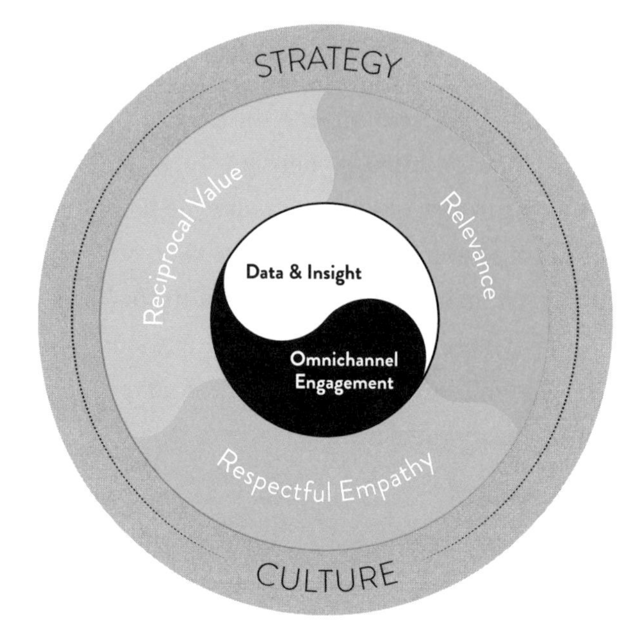

elements that build and strengthen relationships. We call them the three Rs—reciprocal value, relevance, and respectful empathy—and they're the focus of chapters 6, 7, and 8.

- **Reciprocal value forges relationships.** Your customer should never ask, "Why am I getting these messages?" To avoid that question, you must deliver value in every interaction. This is why sports apparel brand Under Armour bought the app family Map My Fitness—to ensure that its messages are useful based on the activities its customers are recording on the app.
- **Relevance strengthens relationships.** For a consumer-first marketer, the key is to maximize relevance in each communication. This means using all available information—the consumers' past purchases, location,

website visits, abandoned shopping carts, social media posts, and even the traffic, pollen count, or weather—to make the message as relevant as possible.

- **Respectful empathy preserves relationships.** The traditional marketing philosophy says you keep messaging the consumer until she buys. In consumer-first marketing, you invert this philosophy, messaging only when you can be helpful. For example, online retailer Fab.com automatically opts customers out of email programs that they never read.

The technology to make consumer-first marketing work **EXISTS NOW.**

These are elements of strategy, but they can only develop if your company's marketing culture is ready to embrace these new ideas. We talk more about culture in chapter 9.

Building the right data foundation, omnichannel capability, and a culture that embraces the three Rs is challenging. But if you succeed at it, as we'll describe in the next five chapters, you'll get a chance to generate the most elusive valuable asset in marketing: customer loyalty.

THE CONSUMER-FIRST MARKETER'S TO-DO LIST

These are your to-dos to get ready for consumer-first marketing:

☐ Identify which of your marketing practices may give consumers the impression that you are a loudmouthed boor.

☐ Evaluate if your organization markets with a product-first, channel-first, or cohort-first focus, and identify the drawbacks that focus is creating.

☐ Evangelize the idea of retaining customers and building relationships.

☐ Identify possible first steps you can make to consumer-first marketing, such as customizing site views and emails based on consumer profiles.

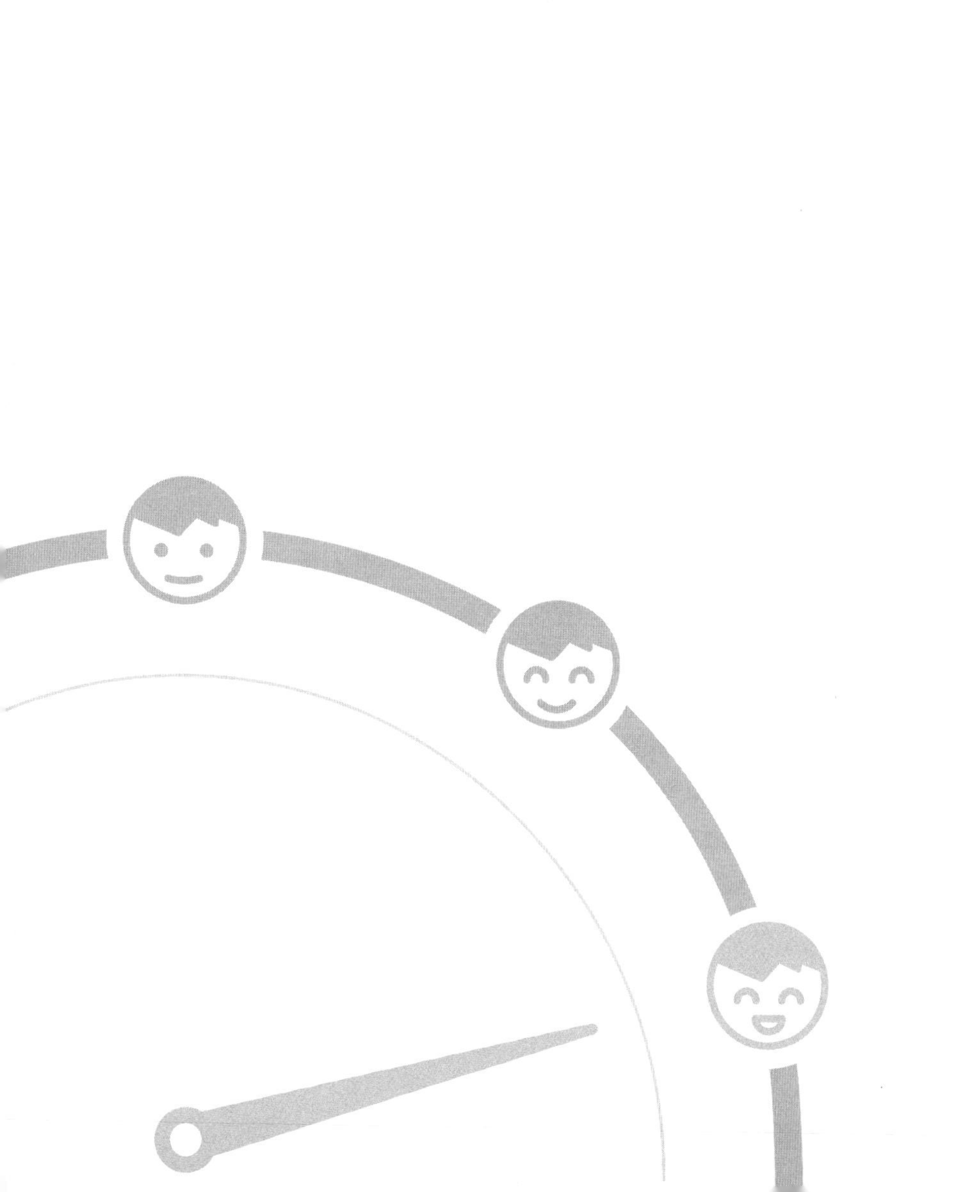

PART 2

THE ELEMENTS OF CONSUMER-FIRST MARKETING

ON SECOND THOUGHT, I'M NOT SURE GIVING YOU MY PERSONAL DATA IS WORTH A 5% DISCOUNT OFF TODAY'S PURCHASE.
ALMOST DONE. GET READY TO TURN YOUR HEAD AND COUGH.
5% OFF
TOM FISH BURNE
© marketoonist.com

Chapter 4

DIVERSE DATA

For Lode Van Laere, marketing is about maximizing relevance. That takes data.

Lode is the chief omnichannel officer at JBC, the largest Belgian clothing retailer. He's worked in petrochemicals, spent time in the Middle East, and been a strategist and a management consultant, but now he is turning his formidable intellect to figuring out exactly what you, the shopper, are looking for and to making sure you know whether JBC has it for you. To fuel his understanding of what you're looking for, he needs to assemble all of JBC's knowledge about you and your habits, combine it with knowledge about what's happening in the world and the current pricing for the inventory that is in stock, and use that intelligence to create an offer with maximum relevance for you, personally. And when JBC's marketing is successful, you, like most of its customers, will come back again and again.

One in three Belgian families shop at JBC—over one million people—and thanks to a popular loyalty program, the company has 24 years' worth of shopping data from those customers. Within that data store are three insights that JBC can apply to determine what you're likely to want next.

First, JBC knows what motivates you to buy. According to Lode, there are two key factors JBC can use to segment different types of shoppers. Some shop on price, whether they buy expensive items, moderately priced ones, or cheaper items. Others are discount-motivated: they tend to wait and buy things when they are on sale. By looking at what was in the shopping basket when you bought in the past—whether the items were more or less expensive relative to similar items and whether you bought them on sale—Lode knows if you are price-sensitive, discount-motivated neither, or both.

By itself, that's not nearly enough to get to maximum relevance. So JBC's marketers also review *when* you shop. If you're typically in the store every couple of months and you've been away for seven weeks, they know you're due back. By analyzing this recency/frequency data, JBC knows exactly when to contact customers and what to say to get them back in the store.

Finally, of course, JBC knows what types of items you bought. Do you shop for kids' clothes, women's clothes, men's clothes, or some combination of those? Based on that knowledge, the company knows what to show you that you're likely to want to see.

JBC's digital marketing team applies these insights, then sends exactly the right message in the language that the customer prefers: French, Flemish, or German. The objective is to get the timing so perfect that the customer will respond, "I was just thinking about that."

Take Brigitta, a hypothetical Flemish-speaking Belgian mom. She's discount-driven and shops for her whole family about once every ten weeks. In the spring, she'll get an email in Flemish about men's sport shorts and kids' trousers, as well as clearance items from last year's collection, just when she's ready to head back into the store.

Or Marie, who speaks French at home. She shops only for her kids, buys high-end clothes, and is in there once a month. So, in August, she'll get a French-language message focused on quality, not on sale prices, featuring some really stylish back-to-school clothes.

Lode is continuing to refine the data that his company collects and the ways he uses it. Tell him the date your kid was born, and he'll send you a message about a free age-appropriate book right around the time you're thinking about birthday presents. And JBC is working on customization based on environmental factors and channels. When the Belgian postal service is on strike and JBC's catalogues can't go in the mail, JBC will send you messages to drive you online to look at product specials, creating a similar experience to the catalog experience. If it's going to rain after a week of clear skies, JBC's marketers will remind you that you might need to buy a raincoat. And unlike most companies, at JBC, if you call the contact center or interact with a salesperson at the point of sale, the reps there know *you*. They'll pull up your profile and treat you the way you ought to be treated based on the information in there.

JBC has already been seeing an increase in the open rates of its emails. But, as Lode says, "The value is in how many people are converting. It's the new million-dollar question: How far can you go in suggestions to a customer that are very personalized and that he or she feels are just right for them?"

Lode uses data very carefully, because the trust of the customer is at stake. "Bottom line," he says, "the information the customer shares with you is the currency she shares with you. The data about what she pays for, you must use it the right way, or she will withdraw that currency from the data bank—take the data out of our system. But if our message to her is relevant, she'll leave it in the data bank and add even more."

THE RIGHT DATA IS CENTRAL TO CONSUMER-FIRST MARKETING

As we described in chapter 3, consumer-first marketing depends on collecting the right data and then using it to power relevant interactions regardless of channel. To get started with this, you must open your mind to new ways of thinking about data.

The data-driven, maximum-relevance marketing strategy Lode Van Laere is executing at JBC is the logical endpoint of a long evolution in marketing. Every marketer is somewhere along the way on that evolutionary timeline, but few have reached the consumer-first marketing techniques at the end of it, as JBC has.

The start of this timeline was in the nineteenth century, when companies knew their customers well (remember the familiar storekeeper from chapter 1?). But companies large and small left that personal and personalized service behind a long time ago in pursuit of scale and efficiency.

By the time computers started arriving at companies in the seventies, personal relationships had mostly evaporated. The company knew you as a name and address. To send you a bill or a catalog, all they needed to know was where you lived and how much you owed them.

Then marketers got a little smarter. They observed what you were buying. You might get a different catalog depending on whether you bought men's or women's clothes, or furniture or fishing rods.

Eventually, marketers began to participate in co-ops that built databases filled with information about what your preferences were. Car companies knew when you'd last bought a car and what kind of car it was. Home improvement retailers and hardware stores learned who was buying drywall or garden supplies.

In the 1990s, the web arrived. With it came the potential of a far more complete set of knowledge about each customer. What had they browsed? What had they clicked on? What did they buy? Marketers began to capture increasingly detailed information. What was their shoe size? Did they like blue suits or gray? Did they rent horror movies or romantic comedies?

The accumulation of all that data has led us to the brink of a big shift. Masses of data, at least in theory, lead to insights. Consumers can spot when marketers use those insights, and they like it.

Consider it from the consumer's point of view. If a marketer knows something about the consumer and doesn't use it, the marketer looks out of touch. In Lode's case, JBC knows which customers are looking for discounts, so its marketers don't bother those customers with other kinds of offers. They know when the customer has just come into the store, so they don't bug her again a week later.

Remember what we said about trusted friends? If you tell your friend something, you expect that friend to remember it the next time she sees you. Your ongoing friendship is a conversation—every interaction fuels it and moves it forward. If your friend ignores what happened between you and just starts shouting indiscriminately, she's no true friend—she's a loudmouthed boor.

If a marketer knows something about the consumer and doesn't use it, the marketer looks OUT OF TOUCH.

We clearly saw these same expectations in our survey of consumers; 46% of them told us they believe companies should use their personal data to provide better service. As we showed in chapter 1, Anticipators share data to get better service and expect companies to understand their needs. And among Fully Entitled consumers, 29% already have higher expectations of companies that are collecting their data.

Smart consumer-facing companies—especially those born on the web—have taken this principle to heart. In our focus groups with consumers, they continually bring up the level of service at Amazon, a company that leverages its knowledge of everything customers have bought so it can recommend other products in the same categories. Netflix observes what you watch and recommends other horror movies, or British police dramas, or sappy romantic comedies starring Hugh Grant. You may believe your brand is so strong that you're immune from consumers' rising expectations. But brands like Amazon and Netflix are ratcheting up the consumer's expectation of relevance. Remember what we said about the transference of entitlement in chapter 1: your customers will increasingly feel entitled to this personalized treatment.

Today, most marketers aren't even close to this level of insight from the data they collect. And that's the problem. Their clumsy attempts are hitting consumers who know—and expect—that the company should do better. If you try to sell them something they just bought, you look stupid. If you pitch them investment products when they have $11 in their bank accounts, you look stupid. If your customer lives in Manhattan, your solicitation to buy a lawn mower will just lead to guffaws.

"You expect everybody to reach the standards that you get used to from companies like Amazon and Tesco. And you won't accept anything less."

KAREN, financial counselor, UK

Customers expect your company to *use* the knowledge it has. That's easy to talk about, but hard to implement. So in this chapter, we'll explain how *the right* data, collected intelligently and used with insight, fuels consumer-first marketing that doesn't seem clumsy and out of touch.

HOW TO THINK ABOUT THE DATA YOU COLLECT

In consumer-first marketing, data has a purpose. You use it to better understand the customer and to put the exact information she's looking for in front of her at the exact moment she is looking for it.

This demands a different perspective on data collection. The key is to collect data that can be brought together at any moment of interaction to deliver the most relevant information to the customer. To start, let's talk about what types of data you should consider collecting, which data is worth collecting, and how you can combine it effectively.

Brands like Amazon and Netflix are ratcheting up the consumer's **EXPECTATION** of relevance.

The key is to collect data that can be brought together at any moment of interaction to deliver the most **RELEVANT** information.

The four types of consumer data

You must widen your aperture. Consumer data can include everything from the consumer's inseam measurement to social media posts, local weather, and the names of her children. At JBC, the key data includes not just purchase history but language preference. There is no limit to the types of data that can fuel a consumer-first marketing effort.

To expand your thinking, consider the four types of data that can make a difference in consumer-first marketing, listed here from the most persistent to the most ephemeral:

1. **Descriptive data.** These are data elements that don't change much over time. This includes demographic data (age, gender, where the customer lives), but it also includes preferences that remain relatively constant: is the customer a sports fan, a book reader, or a churchgoer, for example. Much of this data is accessible through data suppliers like Acxiom, Experian, and Infogroup.

2. **Social connections.** Consumers are not islands. To understand a consumer, it can be helpful to know not just who's in her household, business, and social circle, but also who she's connected with on social media channels. It can also help to know consumers' likes and dislikes, and whether they are social introverts or extroverts.

3. **Relationship history.** This includes how often you interact with the customer, who usually initiates that interaction, the customer's purchase history, whether and when she called customer service, did she have a complaint, and has she visited your website or your

store. Because this history is based on discrete events, it's changing with every transaction. (In the story about Sophia in chapter 3, historical data about Sophia's purchases made her experience far more relevant and personal.)

4. **Situational data.** This is information that changes in the moment—what's today's weather, who won the football match, is there a lot of traffic in a given location, and so on.

> *"If you've looked at something [on the web] and then come back, even if it's many months later, I know that the offer that you see is already matched [to you]. [I think it even] uses the data about how much you earn, so it'll be matched to your salary with that data."*
>
> **ULRICH,** editor, Germany

If you look back at what Lode Van Laere was doing at JBC, you can see all these forms of data coming together. JBC uses descriptive information about its customers' favored language, connection data about the names and ages of her children, relationship history data about how frequently she visits the store, and situational data about whether it's the first sunny day in a while. JBC taps all this information to determine what kind of message is most likely to be helpful and motivating to a consumer at the exact moment she will receive it.

Don't bother with data unless it will change how you interact with consumers

Given the wide variety of potentially useful data, what's worth combining at the moment of interaction?

Unless you can use data to deliver **EXTRA VALUE** to a consumer, don't bother with collecting it.

To answer this question, ask yourself, "As a marketer, what would I do differently if I knew this?" If you can't think of an answer to that question, that data is not useful to you.

How tall your customer is makes a great deal of difference if you're selling suits and none at all if you're selling cooking utensils.

The weather may be crucial for helping customers think of buying patio furniture, but it probably won't get them thinking about pet insurance.

If you can see how the data you are seeking will help you get the right information to a customer at the moment of interaction, then it's worth the effort to capture it and act on it. If not, it's just clutter—more consumer information to store and sift through that's not useful.

Maribel Lopez, founder of Lopez Research, studied this question in detail for her book *Right-Time Experiences*. As she points out, there's been an explosion in potentially available data about consumers, paralleled by an uneasy suspicion on the part of those consumers that their data is being exploited. "People fail to collect enough information about who I am to do the correlation among all my data sources," she says. "In the end, it's not about use of my data. It's about whether they provide me with anything that is relevant."

In the case of JBC, for example, you might think the names and ages of a consumer's children is irrelevant—until you see how the company uses it in its program around the children's birthdays.

You should use similar judgment. Unless you can figure out how to take advantage of the information you're collecting to deliver extra value to a consumer, don't bother with it.

Assemble data at the moment of interaction

Based on our interactions with marketers, it seems that nearly all marketers are locked into a world where data collection is imprisoned by channels. Web systems, email engines, social listening platforms, call-center applications, and point-of-sale systems all capture customer information, but they typically don't talk to each other.

In fact, in any given company, there may be dozens of systems capturing information about the customer. In addition to this, there are other corporate systems that have relevant data for your customer contacts: product information and inventories, store opening hours, and the language ability of associates in each location, for example. And for maximum relevance, you may need other information about the world, like traffic data and weather conditions.

Integrating all that data is a big challenge. As we'll describe in chapter 5, it requires a new kind of architecture for your systems that use the data. And time and again, we've seen companies fail as they attempt to overhaul all their systems to create what they hope will be a 360-degree view of the customer. That's an effort that could cost hundreds of millions of dollars, take years to implement, and end up obsolete as soon as it's completed as customers and companies develop new ways of interacting, like chatbots or virtual reality, and new streams of data, like health information or streaming media.

Whether or not you're pursuing the vision of a 360-degree customer view, your IT department will inevitably be working on various ways to integrate consumer data. That's a necessary activity. But let's be clear: *marketers do not need a single, fully integrated set of customer data to deliver on consumer-first marketing.*

Marketers **DO NOT** need a single, fully integrated set of customer data to deliver on consumer-first marketing.

Each marketing interaction is **DIFFERENT,** even between the same company and the same consumer—history and real-time events change the **CONTEXT.**

Instead, what you need is a system that can tap into these other systems to integrate just the data that's needed, as it's needed.

At the moment you're about to send an offer, you may want the system to check to see which consumers are in the midst of a service issue and filter those customers out.

If there have been ice storms in an area and you sell insurance, the real-time weather in that area may be exactly what you need to determine which homeowners to contact. (Remember how useful local weather information was to Jennifer Stamper at Extra Space Storage as she sent targeted messages to her customers?)

And if you're pitching a new jacket to a consumer, that might be the moment when you check if the customer has in the past bought blue clothes, red ones, or tan ones, and change up the picture on your email.

Here's an analogy: Plato once quoted his fellow Greek philosopher Heraclitus as saying that a man can never step in the same river twice. When the man returns, the water that is flowing by is different, and the man is different as well, so the interaction between the man and the water is inevitably not the same as it was before.

In the same way, each marketing interaction is different, even if it is between the same company and the same consumer. The consumer is different: perhaps she bought something, returned something, or clicked on something. The company is different: perhaps it has new products or new knowledge about what people are looking for. Finally, the conditions are different: perhaps it's St. Patrick's Day or the customer's birthday, the nearest store is about to close, or a different political party is running the country. The interaction in which the company delivers value to that customer must, therefore, be different as well. Only by pulling these data sources together at that moment of interaction can the company determine the best way to deliver value to that customer at that moment.

How personalized marketing pays off

Does using data to deliver personalized marketing and service make a difference in your sales, or your profit? Boston Consulting Group has now answered that question.[1]

In 2017, researchers from BCG examined personalized marketing and service strategies from more than 50 companies across 10 industries. Their findings were provocative. Two-thirds of their respondents said they expected at least a 6% annual increase in revenue from personalization; financial companies, retail grocery chains, and apparel sellers expected a lift of 10% or more. Half of the companies in the survey had dedicated more than 25 of their employees to personalization programs and invested more than $5 million per year in personalization campaigns.

Mark Abraham, one of the authors of the study and a senior partner and managing director at BCG, explains the strategies that companies need to get to work on to benefit from personalization: change their strategic design, build data and analytics capabilities, transform their technology, and enable new ways of working. And he identifies the change in the way the company works as the hardest of these. "Even the piece around who owns the customers is not clear. In most companies, there is not one owner of the customer," he told us. "If you want to communicate to the customer in a way that cuts across the website, the store, the mobile app, there are three separate groups working on that."

But there is a payoff from working toward personalization. "Customers are demanding this," Mark said. "When they are going to Amazon, they don't have to put in all their info and details every single time. When they interact with a brand, they expect the same level of personalization."

Over the next five years, BCG predicts a revenue shift of $800 billion to the one in six companies that are now investing boldly to set themselves apart with successful personalization strategies—and that prediction is limited to only the retail, health care, and financial services sectors. In the economy as a whole, the shift could be even larger.

YOU CAN PROFIT FROM PERSONALIZED MARKETING, JUST AS THESE COMPANIES DID

Personalized marketing seems like it would require a wholesale rethinking of how your company works. And ultimately, the changes that this sort of marketing strategy will make in your company will ripple through your entire strategy.

But it's possible to get started on profiting now by collecting and applying data intelligently (see sidebar).

So let's take a peek at some marketers who used the four kinds of data we mentioned earlier—descriptive, social connections, relationship history, and situational—to achieve better marketing results.

Customer-first marketing starts with descriptive data applied intelligently

Where you live, what size you are, even what type of dog you have—these are key descriptors that marketers use to begin to segment their messages. And that first level of personalization already creates lift in marketing effectiveness.

It's easy to see this with email programs. Allan Levy, the CEO of the advertising agency SellUP, has seen this strategy work over and again in the campaigns he runs for his clients. He segments his clients' customers into buyers and nonbuyers, for example, and then tests different email subject lines, which often show dramatic differences in responses based on this single piece of information. Now his company tests everything—every offer, every subject line, color, photos, and so on—to make sure the messages connect based on buyers' characteristics.

But personalizing email subject lines and content is just the beginning. Here are a few other ideas to get you thinking. Notice how in many of these cases, demographics is only the first level of personalization data; companies add history or social data to supercharge the effectiveness of their programs.

- **Greenpal, a lawn service, customizes its ads to your zip code.** Rather than show the same search ad to everyone in its service area around Nashville, Tennessee, Greenpal customized the message, emphasizing discounts in zip codes with less-affluent homeowners. The customized ads got clicked three times as often and improved conversions by 30%.[2]

- **Stitch Fix builds its business on knowing your exact measurements and preferences.** When you sign up for Stitch Fix, you tell it your measurements, including dress size, waist, collar size, and what parts of your body you prefer to hide or emphasize. Stitch Fix would also like to know if you are pregnant or a mother and what your job is. By itself, the company's knowledge of these vital statistics enables a consumer-first approach to marketing. But the marketers at Stitch Fix add social data, reviewing the consumer's style choices on Pinterest and Instagram, too. As the company said in a financial filing, customers are motivated to share "because they recognize that doing so will result in more personalized and successful experiences."[3] This strategy drove Stitch Fix revenues up tenfold in three years, and the company now boasts 2 million active clients and $1 billion in sales.

- **Unilever's Axe created personalized videos based on customers' preferences.** Unilever's digital agency in Brazil, CUBOCC, worked with the research firm Box1824 to segment consumers based on factors like musical tastes, favorite brands, and consumption preferences.[4] The agency then synthesized over 100,000 personalized versions of a Romeo and Juliet video to advertise Axe deodorant. As a result of this personalized content, viewers were far more likely to watch the brand ads to the very end.
- **Doggyloot uses dog demographics to personalize messages.** The data that matters to your company depends on how your consumers differentiate themselves. At Doggyloot.com, for example, marketers feature photos of either large or small dogs in emails, because matching the picture to the consumer's dog enables those consumers to more easily identify with the marketing message.[5]

Social connection data is a powerful marketing stimulant

Your consumers' connections and friendships allow you to refine your marketing to the next level. With the advent of social networks, those connections are often visible or accessible to marketers. As we described with Stitch Fix, this socially visible data, used carefully, is a potent marketing enhancer. For example:

- **Cadbury's used viewers' personal history to improve relevance and clickthroughs.** If you go to Cadbury's Facebook page in Australia, it creates a personalized video based on your Facebook photos and experiences, then recommends chocolate based on that knowledge. Nine out of ten viewers watched the video to the end, 65% clicked through on the offer, and 33% filled out a contest form and became leads.[6]
- **Paper Style profits by determining women's relationships with each other.** For Paper Style, which sells invitations and other paper goods for weddings, what matters most is whether you're the bride or one of her friends. According to Silverpop's Loren McDonald, Paper Style sent a separate series of emails to each group: brides' emails focused on invitations, bridal party gifts, and thank-you notes, while their friends got details on planning bachelorette parties and gifts for the couple. This strategy increased open rates by 244%, clickthroughs by 161%, and revenue per mailing by 330%.[7]

Mining consumers' histories makes marketing more relevant

Consumers get really frustrated when you fail to consider their history with you. As JBC found out when it put programs in place based on past purchase patterns, it's much easier to appear as a friend when you account for previous interactions. Marketing that ignores that history is tone-deaf—marketing blithely to customers who had problems in the past, or pitching products they just bought, is going to make you seem more like a loudmouthed boor than a loyal friend. In an Accenture study of 1,500 US and UK consumers, 58% of consumers said they are more likely to purchase from a retailer that recommends options based on past purchases.[8] Here are some examples where marketers used their past history with customers to create a better experience:

- **Secured Retirements personalized offers based on how well the company knows you.** Donna Arriaga explains how her marketing agency, Denamico, applied a simple segmentation approach to a database of contacts of its client Secured Retirements, an investment advisor. Previously, the company had sent the same newsletter to its whole database. The new approach added offers to the newsletter: an ebook offer to unqualified leads, an event/workshop registration to those prequalified by marketing, an invitation to an in-person consultation to those prequalified by sales, and an invitation to a client appreciation event or referral request to those who were already customers. This simple segmentation approach boosted email open rates by 43% and clickthroughs by 89%.[9]
- **Wyanoke gives medical providers more of what they want.** Wyanoke is a medical publisher delivering 40 publications to over two million contacts on its email list. But the company succeeds not because of the size of its lists but because of their level of engagement: its contacts are valuable based on how frequently they open emails, click through to content, buy books, or sign up for conferences. Wyanoke reengaged its customers who had gone dormant, popping up a simple request that prompted the customers to indicate what they were most interested in: news, educational materials, books, or conferences. Within 30 minutes of a customer expressing a preference, Wyanoke responded with a customized

offer. Result: over half of those who saw the email interacted with it.[10]

- **EA's player-first strategy uses game-play to optimize offers.** Electronic Arts (EA), maker of games like The Sims, has a massive amount of data based on every move the player makes in its games. It maximizes retention by adjusting the difficulty of the game based on the player's previous activities.[11] The company has built a centralized player database that can build a progressively growing identity for each player.[12] Analytics determine whom to upsell, what offers to make, and how to time those offers depending on where the player is in her gaming lifecycle.

- **STM, the Montreal subway, refined offers based on the trips people took.** Customers who registered with the STM app, called Merci, got offers for cultural, sporting, and entertainment events and coupons.[13] Because STM knew what stations its 1.2 million daily riders visited from records on their subway cards, it could customize the offers to the locations the riders visited and offer greater rewards to the top tier of riders.[14] Merci rapidly became the top lifestyle app in Montreal, and offer redemptions peaked at 47%.[15]

- **Airlines deliver customized service and marketing based on customer histories.** Delta's flight attendants now carry mobile devices that enable them to see customers' frequent flyer statuses or flag problems they may have experienced on past flights so that they can offer more informed and sensitive service to those passengers.[16] And when EasyJet created personalized marketing messages featuring graphics based on the places flyers had visited, compared to more generic messages, those messages proved 14 times as effective in triggering an action in some markets.[17]

- **Global Giving intelligently uses its knowledge of which causes you support.** The charity organization personalized pitches to its mailing list, using pictures of projects that recipients had previously donated to. This customization resulted in a tenfold increase in engagement and contributions.[18]

In-the-moment information can make all the difference

Why collect data that become obsolete quickly? Because acting on that data can be the most powerful marketing stimulant of all. In-the-moment data is, by definition, relevant to the consumer—where she is, what she is doing, what's going on around her, and what she needs.

Here are some other examples of companies that used data dynamically to make marketing more relevant.

- **Disney World helps you waste less time in line.** The Disney Attractions app and the Magic Band that most Walt Disney World visitors wear tell the theme park where you are and what you're doing. The result is a park that configures itself to make your experience as enjoyable as possible. Order food while you're bopping around the park; the restaurant prepares it to be hot and ready right when you get there.[19] If you're waiting in a 45-minute line for your favorite ride, it might virtually hold your place in line while directing you to a ride next door with a far shorter wait. That's an intelligent use of real-time location information.[20]
- **Emirates warmly extends personal connections across long-haul connecting flights.** Emirates passengers are

typically taking long flights between Europe or the US and Asia, connecting in Dubai. On an Airbus A380, these flights actually have a bar and bartender serving first-class and business-class passengers. The bartender on the first leg of a journey will enter information about passengers' particular preferences or problems in a database so that the bartender on the connecting flight can use it to deliver personalized service on the second leg of the journey.[21]

- **The Dutch online retailer Coolblue decreased returns with timely videos.** Coolblue identified a major source of returns: a lot of customers couldn't get their products, often electronics, to work properly. It began emailing links to how-to videos and instructions from a library of 50,000 product videos, timed to appear in the recipient's inbox on the day the product was delivered. Result: 90% fewer calls and emails to customer service and a 30% reduction in returns.[22]
- **John Deere combines weather and location data to keep farmers safe and productive.** If you're a farmer with John Deere farm equipment, the company will use its real-time information about your machines and their locations to suggest ways in which you can use them more efficiently. The platform even enables personalized analysis based on weather forecasts.[23]

THE KEY TO LEVERAGING EFFECTIVE DATA IS TO DEVELOP INSIGHTS FROM IT

Take a close look at these examples, and you'll see that the most powerful ones combine different types of data to deliver the most helpful message in the moment. Whether that's a Stitch Fix suggestion for perfectly fitted, perfectly styled clothes for you, a subway card that generates offers that match where you emerge above ground, or a John Deere harvester app that knows the history of your farm machinery and whether a storm is on the horizon, these applications are setting expectations for the future. At first, people may be startled at how companies use their data to create surprisingly relevant offers. Then they'll come to expect it and rely on it. And then they'll expect your company to live up to the same standard.

If you don't begin to learn how to integrate these data sources in the moment—to find the triggers that enable you to reach someone at just the moment they need something—you're going to lose that customer. It's not just an opportunity to look smart. It's an imperative not to look stupid.

When an airline knows your flight is late and that you are a 100,000-mile flyer but doesn't take the opportunity to get you to your connection, *they look stupid*.

When a retailer uses retargeting ads to try to sell you a product you just bought, *they look stupid*.

When a financial services company tries to sell you a life insurance policy for your husband—who just died a month ago—*they look stupid*.

When UberEats tries to sell you food in New York after you just took an Uber in L.A., *they look stupid*.

A real friend would know better. And that's what we now expect from companies.

Of course, gathering the data is not sufficient. To be really effective, you need an engine to apply it in the channel where the customer is interacting. That's omnichannel thinking, which we discuss in the next chapter.

THE CONSUMER-FIRST MARKETER'S TO-DO LIST

These are your to-dos to improve how you use data for consumer-first marketing:

- ☐ Audit your marketing data; expand your conception of useful data to encompass not just demographics but social connections, the customer's history with you, and ephemeral data about her situation.
- ☐ Evaluate whether the data that you collect, or are considering collecting, helps you serve the customer more precisely.
- ☐ Don't waste time and energy on a mythical 360-degree view of the customer; assemble the data on the fly from diverse sources as you create and deliver marketing messages.
- ☐ Maximize message relevance by adding social, relationship history, and in-the-moment data to what you already know about the customer.
- ☐ Consider ways to improve your personalization with situational data sources like weather, traffic, and inventory.

CARL, YOUR DEODORANT ISN'T WORKING
ONE-TO-ONE MARKETING IS GETTING OUT OF HAND.
TOM FISH BURNE
© marketoonist.com

Chapter 5

OMNICHANNEL ENGAGEMENT

A good friend recognizes you anywhere. Even if you've changed your hair color or just became a new mom. You're different, but you're still *you*. Whether you're on the phone, at a party, or in a dimly lit restaurant, she remembers you—what you're doing, what you're aspiring to, and what you laughed about the last three times you got together.

Can a company do that?

Right now, there are a bunch of companies that deliver that exact experience.

Take Google. When you log into your Gmail, Google remembers everything. It knows which emails you've filed, which ones you've already read, and which ones you've put a star next to—even if you filed them on your PC, read them on your tablet, and used your smartphone to put the stars on them. If you get an email about a flight, the flight appears on your calendar. When you look at Google Maps, it highlights the location of your appointments. When you open the Chrome browser on your tablet, you can see the tabs you had open in Chrome on your Mac. The Google Assistant on your Android phone will even tell you when to leave—allowing for traffic—to get from where you are to the location of your next appointment on time.

Google has figured out all the devices and channels you're using: phones, tablets, smart speakers, thermostats, apps, and browsers. Its products—Gmail, Google Messenger, Google Calendar, Search, YouTube, Chrome, and Android—are all just different ways of interacting with what's important to you. Google learns what's important and makes it transparently available in whatever channel you use to connect with it. Google connects everything, and it never forgets.

It's not just Google. Facebook never loses track of what you've read, what you liked, what you posted on Instagram, and who you're friends with, regardless of what device you use to connect with it. (You may not be happy with who has access to that information, but it's all in there.) And Spotify refines what it plays on your music channels, independent of device, based on which songs you like and which you skip.

Think this kind of thing only works in the virtual world? If you go into one of Amazon's new bookstores—there were 13 of them open as of the end of 2017, with more coming—then Amazon recognizes you when you check out. As you pay with your credit card, it recognizes that you're an Amazon Prime member and gives you the heavily discounted online price. And Amazon remembers what you bought and will prompt you to log in and write a review soon after. Is this sort of experience coming to an Amazon-owned Whole Foods store soon? Almost certainly.

This level of customer knowledge in all channels is not limited to born-online companies like Google, Facebook, Spotify, and Amazon. Even companies like yours, with real-world products, physical locations, distribution chains, and customer service operations, are implementing them. Remember, regardless of what kind of business you run, your entitled customers don't see those distinctions between digital and real-world interactions. They know that companies like Amazon recognize them no matter where they show up and deliver an experience that accounts for all the previous interactions they had, every post, click, rating, and purchase. And they're going to expect the same thing from you.

> **To deliver consumer-first marketing, you need BOTH diverse data and omnichannel engagement.**

It's time you figured out how to deliver on that expectation.

THE CENTRAL AND INTERDEPENDENT ELEMENTS OF CONSUMER-FIRST MARKETING

You need two things to deliver on consumer-first marketing. The first is data, as we described in the previous chapter. And the second is omnichannel engagement: the ability to deliver a consistent experience across channels based on that data. In this chapter, we'll focus on how to leverage data to deliver a consistent omnichannel experience.

Consider what a company like Google must put in place to deliver a consistent experience. Google's data includes who you are, what emails you've read, what tabs you have open on Chrome, what's in your schedule, what ads you've clicked on, what's stored on your Google Drive, where you drove using Google Maps, and where you typically go at different times of day.

But that data is not sufficient. When you log into Gmail or Google Maps or look at your schedule on your phone, those applications must instantly access all the relevant data to deliver the right experience to you. The Google Schedule on your phone, the Chrome tabs on your tablet, and the Gmail display on your computer are all just windows into that experience. Google's engineers have worked hard to integrate that experience so that no matter where you are, no matter what you are doing, and no matter what device you are doing it on, you appear to be interacting transparently with Google and your data. Google recognizes you anywhere and treats you accordingly, like a friend.

To understand the relationship between data and omnichannel engagement, consider the yin and yang of Taoist philosophy. The light and dark sides of the yin-yang symbol are interconnected and independent, complementary elements that combine to form reality. In the same way, data and omnichannel engagement are complementary elements of consumer-first marketing. In any given interaction, the data is a necessary element that the company must bring to bear to make that interaction as relevant as possible—in whatever channel the consumer has chosen to interact with. But during that interaction, the consumer generates new data, which the company must store for the future.

Steve Furman, of Discover Financial, explains how it looks from his company's perspective. "We think about omnichannel as the ability for a customer to avail themselves of any connection point they would have with us. They should be able to do whatever they want to do in any of those channels. It is about how you can start in channel A and finish in channel B. Like bill pay: if I have set up a payee on the website, I can easily pay that merchant from the mobile."

> **Data and omnichannel engagement are INTERCONNECTED, INTERDEPENDENT elements of consumer-first marketing.**

Here's another example. Suppose I am a customer of American Airlines. The airline knows a lot about me: all the flights I have ever taken, what seats I sat in, whether the flights left and landed on time, how many frequent flyer miles I have, and whether my status is Gold, Platinum, or Executive Platinum. It knows if I have an American Airlines credit card. It knows how many times I have called in to change or check on reservations and whether those reservations were made on Expedia, through a travel agent, or directly with the airline.

It brings the data to bear in every interaction. As we described in chapter 3, when I log into the American Airlines app on the day of a flight, it tells me how long it will take to get to the airport based on my location and invites me to check in. If I call the airline to change the reservation because of a snowstorm heading for the East Coast, it recognizes me from my phone number and shows that reservation to the customer service agent so that she is ready to help me make a switch. And once I'm off the phone, everything we did feeds back into my data with the company, so the next time I call, check the app, visit the website, or check in for a flight, all that information can make the company's interaction with me smarter.

Imagine how helpful this is when I call the airline. And then imagine what it would be like if I called and the agent treated me like a nobody, despite 25 years of flying with American and hundreds of flights.

Author Steven Van Belleghem, a keen observer of marketing trends, believes we're not yet at the perfect scenario where marketers "know and understand your context." To most marketers, the data is "just a number of facts that they try to use in an isolated way." The perfect omnichannel future isn't here yet. But that's no excuse not to get started on developing it.

Sure, in most companies, the data sources are not integrated, and the algorithms cannot deliver a perfect set of flawless interactions in every channel. But the world is moving in the direction of Google and Facebook and Amazon, a world where those interactions are smart and consistent and relevant based on everything the company knows about me. Whatever kind of company you have and whatever your current systems for interacting with customers look like, this is the expectation your entitled consumers are bringing. You'd better figure out how to meet those expectations.

A NEW APPROACH TO CUSTOMER JOURNEYS

Customer experience—the totality of how customers engage with your company—is crucial to a company's success. If customers have a great experience—that is, if they get what they're looking for every step of the way with your company and don't encounter frustrating obstacles—they're much more likely to become loyal customers.

There's a whole science now developing around customer experience and how to optimize it. But, for marketers in particular, the traditional view of customer experience may be getting in the way of delivering relevance in every channel, based on all the data the company can bring to bear.

The traditional view of customer experience begins with a *customer journey*—a series of steps the customer takes to get from point A (say, never having heard of your brand) to point B (say, buying your product). To improve that customer journey, you are supposed to create a "journey map": a diagram of how the customer gets from here to there. As author and Frog Design veteran Adam Richardson describes it in an article on the *Harvard Business Review* online, "A customer journey map is a very simple idea: a diagram that illustrates the steps your customer(s) go through in engaging with your company, whether it be a product, an online experience, retail experience, or a service, or any combination."[1]

This exercise of journey mapping is definitely a useful way to identify sticking points within the customer's experience. For example, the financial services company Barclays Africa used journey mapping to examine how customer service agents handled complaints. It created a map of that journey featuring all the steps and pitfalls in detail.[2] It then turned that map into a learning tool that it used to train agents to quickly identify the root cause of customers' problems. And, as Forrester found, after the customer experience function itself, the group most likely to be involved in these journey-mapping initiatives was marketing.[3]

The problem is that marketers use the same term to mean something very different. In most marketing departments, what's actually happening is a distorted caricature of this disciplined journey-mapping process. The "journeys" that marketers typically focus on are often discrete and linear marketing campaigns, such as an onboarding program, retention campaign, or win-back initiative. For example, they may analyze the "abandoned cart" journey, a sequence of steps that happens after a customer abandons her shopping cart on a website. Or they may look at an "onboarding" journey, a series of messages they send after the first time someone buys a product from them. The problem with these journeys is that they assume the consumer will follow a defined path; as the possible branch-

Many marketing departments imagine a distorted, campaign-based **CARICATURE** of actual customer journeys.

es on that path ramify, the marketer struggles to manage all the permutations. Ultimately, the problem is that the marketers still act as if they are in control. They are undertaking marketing campaigns and treating them as if they are journeys. They're not thinking consumer-first.

Any true customer experience professional will tell you why these "journeys" fail. First of all, they are journeys as described from the perspective of a marketer, not a consumer. In understanding an actual customer journey, we start with the consumer's motivation (for example, pay my bill) and follow that customer as she attempts to accomplish her goal. But no actual consumer says, "I'm on a journey to become interested in, and then eventually buy, this lawn mower" (or gym subscription, or insurance policy, or sport utility vehicle). The customer doesn't even perceive her potential interest in, and interaction with, your company *as* a journey—that's a construct forced on her activities by marketers.

As the marketing experts at Retention Science describe,

> The whole point of the [marketing] funnel was that the competition narrowed down as you went through the process; people started with one big group, and then eliminated brands until they were left with the winner. In stark contrast, consumers today take matters into their own hands: By looking up reviews and researching online, asking for opinions and referrals, it's now the norm to add one or two options after eliminating a few from the original selection...Consumers are no longer evaluating or selecting their purchases by how much your marketing message is able to

> sway them one way or the other. It's now a much more complicated conversation, with consumers doing their own research and independently comparing and contrasting. It's one reason that roughly 70% of purchases are abandoned at the shopping cart: Shoppers often start looking for external product reviews before pulling the trigger, and just as often disappear down the black hole of Googling.[4]

Whether it's approached from the traditional customer experience perspective or from the marketing campaign perspective, journey mapping simply cannot cope with trying to make a generalization about decisions and pathways to purchase that are that diverse and variable.

So put the journey mapping aside for a moment—or use it, as the professionals do, to identify and streamline only the most *common* experiences that your customers have. When it comes to consumer-first marketing, you need a different approach, one that can cope with the thousands of possible paths that your customers may be taking at any given moment. We call that approach *adaptive customer engagement*.

ADAPTIVE CUSTOMER ENGAGEMENT

In an adaptive customer engagement strategy, the marketer's job is, at any given moment, in whatever channel the customer is interacting with, to deliver to the customer exactly what is most likely to be of help or interest.

This takes place in a repeating cycle of three steps:

Recognize. Identify the customer regardless of channel. Bring to bear all relevant data about that customer.

Connect. Continue the conversation across channels. Whether the customer is in a store, on your website, viewing an ad, using your app, reading email, or calling or chatting with your customer service staff, use the information from the "recognize" phase to deliver exactly what the customer is most likely to respond to or perceive as helpful.

Learn. Use every interaction to gather more data. Prepare yourself for the next interaction by learning as much as possible about the customer and how she engaged at each previous interaction.

These steps are essential to go from the marketing overload we described in chapter 2 to the consumer-first marketing model that entitled consumers expect. If you don't want to behave like a loudmouthed boor, you need to know who you're interacting with, extend the connection with each interaction, and deepen the relationship by learning more.

You could see this clearly in Sophia's story from chapter 3. When Sophia gets a push message from the retailer Hailey's on her way to work, she taps "Maybe later." The push message was just for her (recognize), the conversation was continuing on her phone (connect), and when she taps "maybe later," she provides more data: the data that she won't respond to push messages on weekday mornings (learn). When she shows up in the store to pick up a product, the store associate identifies Sophia on a point-of-sale iPad (recognize) and responds with personalized suggestions (connect), and Hailey's acknowledges and learns from her acceptance of the new products (learn).

Are customers ready for these cross-channel interactions? Increasingly, they are, especially entitled consumers. As we shared in chapter 1, our surveys show that more than half of consumers wanted to see boarding passes to pop up on their mobile devices when they arrived at the airport, to check into hotels without going to the desk, or to get suggestions on better prices when shopping with a bank card. Among Fully Entitled consumers, the levels of acceptance for these interactions are even higher (see table 8).

So let's take a look at these three stages of interactions and how companies can accomplish them.

> In adaptive customer engagement, the marketer's job is, at **ANY GIVEN MOMENT,** to deliver to the customer exactly what is most likely to be of help or interest.

Recognize: Identify the customer regardless of channel

Your friend recognizes you regardless of the context in which you show up—at a party, in a restaurant, or at your front door. Can companies recognize customers in the same way?

It takes work, but increasingly, the answer is that they can.

For outbound messages from the company, recognition is easy. You know who you're emailing or sending a text message to. But what about when the customer shows up where you are?

Customers expect to be recognized and receive personalized service when they enter a retail store with their smartphone.

You can recognize them on your website if you give them a reason to log in—for example, to order, return, or check on a product. That's how cookies work: put a digital cookie on the customer's computer, and the next time she shows up, if she has identified herself and given you permission to remember her, you know who she is. The same cookies apply when the customer is browsing an ad on another site. The relationship you created through the visit to your site extends to the ad (see sidebar).

Table 8: Entitled consumers are ready for omnichannel experiences

	CONSUMER GROUP				
WOULD YOU BE HAPPY IF...	ALL	INDIF-FERENTS	ANTICI-PATORS	DEMAND-ERS	FULLY ENTITLED
An airline popped up my boarding pass on my mobile device as soon as I arrived at the airport.	55%	40%	56%	54%	71%
A hotel allowed me to check in to my room on my mobile device without having to go to the reception desk.	52%	38%	53%	52%	65%
My bank or credit card company interrupted me when I was about to buy something to point out better pricing elsewhere.	51%	34%	53%	51%	69%
An online store sent a message before my shopping cart expires.	48%	34%	51%	45%	64%
A movie theater sent me information about the screen location and a refreshments coupon when I arrived.	48%	33%	54%	43%	63%

	CONSUMER GROUP				
WOULD YOU BE HAPPY IF...	ALL	INDIF-FERENTS	ANTICI-PATORS	DEMAND-ERS	FULLY ENTITLED
My insurance company could track my driving behavior and adjust my premiums accordingly.	43%	30%	46%	37%	58%
My doctor could track my fitness activity and what I eat to provide health advice.	42%	28%	49%	35%	59%
A store I was passing by sent me an alert about a sale.	39%	25%	46%	29%	57%
I never had to take my wallet out of my pocket to pay for things—my phone or watch should be enough.	30%	18%	39%	23%	45%
My refrigerator ordered food when I was running low.	29%	17%	35%	22%	43%

Source: Entitled Consumer Survey.
Base: 2,000 US consumers and 1,000 consumers in each of five European countries.

But recognizing the consumer can extend much further than this.

In a store, you may ask the customer for her phone number or request a loyalty card. Or you may recognize the customer because of your app on her phone, which recognizes that she's entered your real-world location.

If a customer calls in, you can recognize her from her phone number. Delta, United, and American Airlines already do this for frequent flyers calling their service numbers, using the information to deliver automated information on upgrades and flight delays.

There are "federated" identity owners, such as Google and Facebook. When a customer logs into a site by using one of these IDs, you can recognize her even if she hasn't logged into your system. Verizon's Oath, made up of the combination of AOL and Yahoo, provides yet another possible way of identifying anyone who logs in.

These methods can break down on mobile devices, where the customer's identification doesn't persist across apps and browsers. But even there, identity methods are spreading. Providers such as Drawbridge, Oracle, and Tapad combine identifiable qualities like screen resolution, device type, operating system, location, Wi-Fi network, and even clock accuracy into a device identifier. Although this device identification doesn't always work, when these providers are able to spot a returning customer, their identifications are typically at least 90% accurate.[5]

Add these methods together, and you'll often be able to recognize the customer regardless of whether she's showing up at your site, on your Facebook page, or in your store. If you don't recognize her, you can ask her to log into Facebook or Google, provide a phone number, or swipe a loyalty card. Or, as Amazon does in its Amazon bookstores, spot the returning customer based on her credit card.

Managing identity

How do marketers ensure that an individual to whom they've mailed an offer, sent an email, or received a site visit from is one person, not three different people? And how do they determine whether J. Smith, John Smith, and John L. Smith are the same person or different people? The easy answer is that they have to invest in identity management as part of their customer data management process. But as marketers interact with consumers with increasing frequency, across more touchpoints, and with different devices, keeping track of identity is far easier said than done.

Marketers can start by building anonymous profiles. When a new or unknown visitor arrives at your website, begin to build a profile based on the cookie ID (which would indicate that the browser has previously been used to visit your site and might include information about what they viewed), IP address (which can indicate location), and device and browser fingerprints (information about which browser a consumer is using, the operating system, and plugins and settings).

Collectively, this identity data helps form what is known as a pseudonymous profile, and together with the visitor's in-session activity (which sections of a site she visits and which products she seems to be interested in), this data can enable you to build a temporary profile of the visitor and begin to serve her more relevant content. You can further nail down identity with third-party vendors that offer cross-device identity solutions such as Drawbridge, Oracle, and Tapad. Although these solutions won't identify who the individual is, they will allow marketers to continue a single conversation with her channels and devices.

To build a relationship with the person behind the browser or device, however, you need to know who she is. Once the visitor goes on to register or purchase from the site (during the first session or a future one), then you can associate that previously pseudonymous profile with a new or existing customer profile and understand the customer's full set of relationships with your company.

In a universal consumer profile, which we discuss in more detail later in this chapter, marketers assign a personal ID to each individual customer. This can range from an email address, phone number, or loyalty number to a unique string of letters and numbers. And whichever is used as the primary identity, all of the other elements act as nodes to link the data together. Some marketers use postal addresses, for example, as key nodes for linking data in a profile over time. They can also use third-party identifiers—from companies like Acxiom, Oracle, Google, or Facebook—to link to a profile, making it richer still.

Connect: Continue the conversation across channels

While many companies have figured out how to wire together their digital channels, the biggest challenge remains connecting physical channels like stores, bank branches, and theme parks with digital channels in a way that puts the consumer's needs first. But when companies can do this, the results are powerful. Here are some examples of companies that got it right and reaped the benefits:

- **Disney Parks & Resorts is the master of omnichannel engagement.** Disney starts by encouraging you to plan your trip with its online "My Disney Experience" tool, which is accessible as a mobile or desktop website or as an app. But, as we described in chapter 3, it extends that experience into the real world with a Magic Band that you wear on your wrist, which comes in a package that you receive just before your trip. The Magic Band unlocks your room, gets you into the park, allows you to pay at restaurants, and generally ensures a tight connection between the plan you made ahead of time and your experience in the park.

- **Retailers are using in-store technology to give customers just what they want.** The in-store/digital connection challenges retailers, but those who have figured it out are profiting. Neiman Marcus recognizes what size shoes and clothes you search for online, then tells you which nearby stores have those sizes in stock and emails you about brands you've clicked on.[6] Value City Furniture lets employees in the store pull up and review or add to your online shopping list, and then the company emails you to nudge you along on purchases you've let languish—strategies that have nearly tripled the store's revenue associated with emails.[7] Crate & Barrel tried putting tablets and scanners in its Skokie, Illinois, store; after you use one to build a wish list, the company emails the list to you and uses browser cookies to remind you about planned purchases with retargeted ads. That trick boosted its sales in Skokie by 10%. And at Fabletics, which began as an online brand, employees at the company's 24 stores scan items as a customer goes into a fitting room, and their tablets suggest accessories to match.[8]

- **Banks are integrating the experience across phones, branches, and sites.** It's commonplace at banks like Bank of America for local bank staffers and phone service representatives to have access to all your history and help you complete your goals. TBC bank in the nation of Georgia took things even further with a tool called FICO origination manager, allowing customers to start a loan application on the phone, then complete it at an ATM, kiosk, or local bank branch. As a result, the loan approval rate went from 50% to 70%, even as the cost to the bank to originate a loan dropped by half.[9]

These types of integrated experiences make it more likely that consumers will stick with the companies that offer them. When American Express notices you've booked a trip on its credit card and lets you know it's fine to use the card in the country you're visiting, it makes you want to book more trips using your AmEx.

Learn: Use every interaction to gather more data

The key to these omnichannel successes is to complete the loop, using every customer experience to learn more. Disney uses your adventures in the park to build a profile of what you've done and what you might want to do in the future. Crate & Barrel adds your activities in its store in Skokie to your profile, becoming smarter about what you'll want on your next purchase. The company that builds a virtuous cycle of collecting data, delivering an intelligent experience across channels, and then learning more for the next time is on its way to creating loyalty that matches the lock-in that Google and Facebook have achieved.

PREPARING YOUR SYSTEMS FOR OMNICHANNEL ENGAGEMENT

As enticing as the vision of omnichannel engagement is, it takes a lot of hard work to make it possible. To get it right, you will need to rethink your approach to three things: how you manage customer data, how you manage the content that you deliver, and the methods you use to decide what to send to customers in each interaction.

We learned from marketers who have gone through this transition. Jim Davis, vice president of global omnichannel at the footwear and fashion company Deckers, recalls the cultural and technical changes the company needed to overcome to build a better way to take advantage of all the data it had. "We reorganized for omnichannel to deliver better customer experience. We focus more on infrastructure that everyone in marketing can tap into to control the planning and go-to-market process," he explained. "We're now changing business processes, changing how marketing links with the way we go to market with products, and thinking about audience first rather than which publications to target. And we're doing it on a global scale."

The key to omnichannel success is to complete the loop, using every customer experience to LEARN MORE about the customer.

A new data architecture manages the mass of unstructured data

In the previous chapter, we talked about the value of diverse data. But to take advantage of that data for omnichannel engagement, you need new ways to manage it.

Big Data experts talk about the explosion in the volume, variety, and velocity of data flooding into companies. Volume: digital customer interactions mean companies now have terabytes of moment-to-moment data about inventory, deliveries, returns, and customer activities. Variety: the data now includes every website click, every tap on a mobile app, every ad you see, and every customer service interaction—plus web activity like social media posts. And velocity: these new types of data are flooding into companies every moment. Within this deluge of Big Data is the in-

To make omnichannel engagement work, you must **RETHINK** how you manage data, how you manage content, and how you decide what to send in each interaction.

sight you need to deliver on the promise of consumer-first marketing.

It's no longer enough to just capture traditional structured data—what someone responded to, bought, or returned—in traditional tables and databases. Unstructured data from all customer interactions adds complexity in a way that marketing databases weren't built to cope with. Even so, marketers are already embracing Big Data in two key ways: to enable programmatic advertising for online display and video and as a foundation for relationship marketing.

Managing all this takes a whole new viewpoint on the architecture for data and how to use it. Without that new way of thinking, you'll never be able to build marketing that delivers the exact right connection, based on all available data, at the exact moment the consumer is ready for it.

The new and innovative approach to managing customer knowledge has arrived in the form of a customer data platform, or CDP. As David Raab, founder of the Customer Data Platform Institute describes it, a CDP is "a marketer-managed system that creates a persistent, unified customer database that is accessible to other systems." These systems provide a single platform to ingest data, then store and retain the metadata (that is data about the data, such as where it was captured, what changes were made to it, or how it is formatted). The system lets marketers examine this data in aggregate or at the customer level through a form of universal consumer profile, and it also exposes the data to any external system for use by the marketer or their agencies. Advanced CDPs enable companies to manage unstructured and structured data and to capture data from any channel.

The critical thing is not necessarily to run out and license a CDP to plug into your existing and crowded marketing technology stack but to make sure you and your team have access to all the important functionality outlined above and that the CDP can function smoothly with the other tools you are using.

To manage diverse data, you need a **CUSTOMER DATA PLATFORM** that creates a persistent, unified customer database that is accessible to other systems.

Atomized content fuels the right set of messages

Marketers spend millions of dollars to develop a marketing tagline or hook. They cannot dilute it by using different brand identities for different customers. But within that broader identity, they can alter the look and feel of their communication to make each interaction more relevant for the recipient. Is the potential car buyer into performance, safety, or the environment? Is the hotel guest a business or leisure traveler, focused on adventure or relaxation, or looking to hit the slopes or the sand? Or is a prospective college student concerned with future debt, Greek life, prestige, or the right career launchpad? The images that marketers use in their communications are just as important as the message.

For example, at Honda, messages to customers look different depending on whether those customers are focused on performance, environment, or safety. The images and the language match the customer's past interactions with the brand.

Disney Parks & Resorts uses atomized content even more effectively. When it sends a welcome kit to the home of a family that has just booked a major vacation, every line of text and every image is tailored based on what the company knows about the family: the number of children in the household, their ages, and their gender, for example. Sending images of princesses to teenage boys or haunted houses to six-year-old girls would literally send the wrong message.

> *"If you have my data, figure it out."*
> **RAGNA,** web producer, Sweden

To deliver the right message with the right image requires marketers to break down their content into increasingly smaller pieces that can be assembled on the fly based on their knowledge of the consumer and her situation. The customer is in a unique and differing state at any given moment, just as Heraclitus' man who cannot step in the same river twice. As a result, there is a set of best images and messages for that customer at that unique moment.

Your web content management and email platform providers can probably handle personalizing content on the web or in an email. But that's not enough. You need to embrace a solution that can assemble your atomized content in real time wherever you are interacting with a customer, based on what you know about her need in her specific context.

A marketing decision engine generates the right message for any given interaction

A marketing decision engine uses contextual information, machine learning, and continuous testing to determine and deliver the optimal interaction. By its nature, the decision engine is continuously improving, optimizing its decisions by observing which interactions drive the highest degree of engagement.

The decision engine begins with descriptive analytics—understanding customers as individuals or in distinct groups through look-alike modeling. Then it adds sophistication, carefully examining every element of customer interactions and determining which ones lead to the most productive connections, a discipline called multitouch attribution. Ultimately, it uses machine learning to build models that prescribe the activity that will produce the best outcomes.

To deliver the right message with the right image, you must break down your content into INCREASINGLY SMALLER pieces that can be assembled on the fly.

The resulting decision engine is a single place to make decisions on the optimal message and content for each customer at the point of each interaction. It brings together all the elements we've mentioned in the last two chapters: masses of diverse data, atomized content, analyses of customer journeys, techniques for recognizing customers, optimized interactions, and learning from the results. It keeps getting smarter. And its ultimate objective is to deliver, at any given moment, with all possible context, and in whatever channel the customer is using, the most productive possible interaction.

As you embrace omnichannel, you'll notice a strange phenomenon—until you become an expert, you'll find that the more you focus on harmonizing across channels, the less sophisticated you will be in each individual channel. You can offset this concern by embracing in-channel innovation while simultaneously expanding your omnichannel capability. For example, in the email channel, open-time personalization—which we described briefly when explaining Intercontinental Hotel Group's use of weather in its emails—allows you to update content at the time an email is opened and read. This allows marketers to make the best decision at the time they are sending the email but also to update the

A marketing decision engine uses contextual information, machine learning, and continuous testing to determine and deliver the **OPTIMAL** interaction.

content the recipient sees when she opens it if the situation or circumstances change. This ability to deliver live content often includes countdown clocks, updated jackpots, and live scores, but it can just as easily change because you are aware that the recipient has now seen the original content in another channel, for example, and you wish to continue and evolve the conversation—just as a friend would.

When omnichannel engagement works, it's powerful, not just in terms of the revenue it delivers but in terms of stronger and more robust relationships with customers (see sidebar). A customer who receives these sorts of customized interactions will perceive herself to be interacting with the company, not with a series of disconnected channels and clumsy sales pitches—exactly the sort of interaction that Google is currently delivering but extended out into the real world. And that customer will perceive the company as she does a friend who remembers her, knows her, and knows just what she needs in any given moment. That's where loyalty comes from.

The role of AI in consumer-first marketing

Think about your best friend. You know her age, gender, size, where she lives, and what car she drives; you know her health issues, religion, and interests; you might know if she is planning to have a baby, to change jobs, or to remodel her home; you probably know many members of her immediate and extended family, and you might know some of her lifelong friends, work colleagues, and college pals. Every time you interact with them, you naturally incorporate all that knowledge into your conversation without thinking about it.

Similarly, as we discussed in the last chapter, effective marketers also must capture relationship history and situational data and combine it with descriptive and social data as they interact with consumers. Bringing all that data to bear as it's needed is a big challenge.

People in marketing or customer service can't always instantly access exactly the right information when interacting with a customer. For years we've used databases to store customer information, mined it to predict who might respond to what offer, and targeted them. But the volume of data that companies capture today and the consumer expectation of relevance and value (which we'll discuss in greater depth in later chapters) render traditional database approaches obsolete. The solution is artificial intelligence (AI), and it's far more than a buzzword. AI is the study of how to make machines intelligent, enabling them to "learn" based on patterns rather than utilizing preprogrammed rules. Although the term "artificial intelligence" dates back to the 1950s, it is in the past few years that marketers—and the vendors that sell to them—have really started to explore how AI and machine learning (ML) can work for them in practice. Now, however, the AI flywheel is turning; 84% of marketing organizations are implementing or expanding AI and machine learning in 2018.[10]

Marketers have been using AI for some time, even if they don't realize it. Most search engine marketing, brand/trademark monitoring, and programmatic advertising vendors use AI to drive their systems. Increasingly, though, marketers are gaining direct access to leverage AI and ML to inform their customer interactions and relationship efforts. For example:

- Recommendation engines apply AI to select content based on past behavior of similar users (collaborative filtering), better predicting the next best offer/content to show a consumer.

- *Content creation engines, automated customer service systems, and chatbots are using natural language processing (NLP) to perform contextual searches, streamline processes, and answer questions.*

- *Speech recognition—not just on the telephone IVR systems but also via smart devices—leverages artificial neural networks and models called hidden Markov models that predict the likeliest words. This intelligence enables these systems to recognize and translate spoken language into text.*

- *Facial recognition that recognizes or verifies a person is already finding use in marketing applications from skin care to travel. Warby Parker uses Apple's Face ID to allow buyers to "see" themselves wearing different pairs of glasses.*

While the use cases will continue to expand and become more mainstream, we believe the key for marketers is to determine the respective roles of humans and machines. There are some things that machines do better (evaluating massive amounts of data in short timeframes, for example) and some things that they will never do as effectively as people (like showing empathy). As part of your planning for the next wave of marketing, you have to determine the level of investment you want to make in machine learning and AI and where you want to invest in hiring and training team members who can best interact with these machines, because together, they will deliver the best experience to your customers.

THE CONSUMER-FIRST MARKETER'S TO-DO LIST

These are your to-dos to prepare for omnichannel engagement:

☐ Stop imagining customer journeys as generic or as campaigns; real customer journeys are much more detailed and complex than that.

☐ Architect a customer data platform that can access diverse sets of customer data, and make the data available to other systems; make sure you can manage your data yourself, removing dependencies on IT or other groups outside marketing.

☐ Atomize your content so you can deliver different messages based on the consumer who is receiving them and her context.

☐ Learn from each interaction; use the knowledge to improve the experiences you deliver to customers.

☐ Leverage a marketing decision engine that uses AI to deliver the right message to each consumer in the right moment and channel.

WAIT, I MAY HAVE A CARD SHOWING MY LOYALTY TO WHATEVER STORE THIS IS
LOYALTY POINTS
6
TOM FISH BURNE
© marketoonist.com

Chapter 6

RECIPROCAL VALUE FORGES RELATIONSHIPS

A few years ago, as I (Dave) was traveling to Ireland, I saw ads in New York's JFK airport suggesting that T-Mobile, the US mobile phone operator, would no longer charge for mobile data usage when customers were overseas. Despite being a longtime customer, I was so skeptical that I tracked down the relevant explanation on T-Mobile's website, went over it with a fine-tooth comb, and took screen captures of the pages in case I had to fight any charges. But T-Mobile was true to its word. There were no data charges for the time I spent overseas.

A few months later I received an email explaining that my monthly bill would drop by $14. I had been paying for unlimited international texting for myself and my wife. T-Mobile was no longer charging for overseas texts, so it dropped the fee.

What kind of a company gives up lucrative fees?

One that continually searches for value for its customers. These moves are part of T-Mobile's "Un-carrier" strategy. As T-Mobile CEO John Legere explained, the Un-carrier strategy is about "finding and solving customer pain points in an attempt to fix a stupid, broken, arrogant industry."[1]

The wireless carrier business is filled with company-first strategies. It has locked people into contracts, then created every possible fee imaginable: upgrade fees, roaming charges, data overage fees, fees for sending texts beyond some limit, and most importantly, early termination fees. Once you have a mobile customer, the traditional industry wisdom goes, you need to get every dollar you can out of her. This approach boosts margins. But it creates resentment and a strong desire for customers to switch to somebody that won't screw them over.

T-Mobile is happy to be that somebody. One of its first Un-carrier moves was to get rid of lock-in contracts, and it even offered to buy you out of your contract with another carrier. Among other promotions, it has offered:

- faster, cheaper, and more frequent phone upgrades;
- free international roaming (the promotion that saved me so much money);
- unlimited talk minutes and texting;
- free tryouts of the T-Mobile network on a loaner phone;
- free music streaming;

- free text messages and voicemail over Wi-Fi while on flights;
- free streaming video for Netflix, Hulu, Amazon, and many other services; and finally,
- ending all limits on data plans, bill credits for customers who use less data, and a commitment never to alter any promised aspects of the service plans in the future.

As I heard Peter DeLuca, SVP of brand advertising and communications for T-Mobile USA, explain at an Ad Age Digital Conference, the company's approach is rooted in customer understanding. Essentially, T-Mobile looked at the major pain points that customers had with their carriers and sought to address them, even if those solutions undermined traditional revenue streams for a mobile operator.

This focus on value has paid off. As the fourth-place mobile operator in 2012, T-Mobile's market share had been plummeting, reaching a low of about 8%.[2] But since the debut of the consumer-first Un-carrier strategy, its share has nearly doubled, and it has moved into third place (see figure 8).[3] T-Mobile has added more than 39 million customers over the last five years, mostly taken from market leaders AT&T and Verizon, carriers that in turn have been forced to match many of T-Mobile's offers.[4] T-Mobile's stock price rose 198% between March 2013 and March 2018, while all of its major competitors have remained flat or declined.

T-Mobile, like other companies that take a consumer-first approach, figured out how to establish a relationship of reciprocal value with its customers. It introduced offers, processes, and benefits that were valuable to consumers, even if those changes threatened the traditional way to do business in the wireless industry. Some of its changes required significant legal, financial,

Figure 8: US retail wireless subscription market share

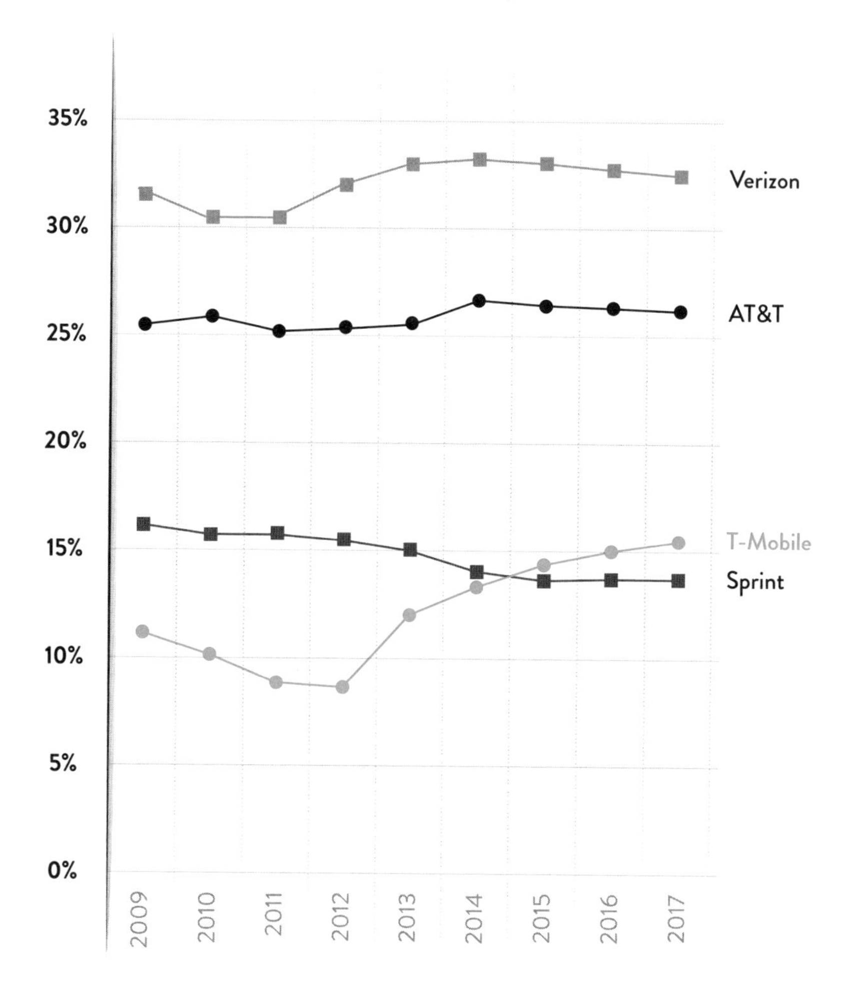

Source: Data from Strategy Analytics.

operational, or technological effort. Some made it easier for customers to leave. But customers stayed, because in contrast to its competitors, T-Mobile focused on creating value for those customers rather than on locking them in and squeezing more money out of them.

THE IMPERATIVE—AND ENDLESS—SEARCH FOR CUSTOMER VALUE

When John Legere was considering taking over leadership of T-Mobile in 2012, the company was not only in fourth place in the US, it was in decline. At the start of his first interview for the CEO position, "right after hello," as he described it, he told the executive from T-Mobile's parent company that he thought there was only one way the company could fail: "Do exactly what you're doing—nothing." That is, keep behaving like every other mobile carrier.

There was no choice but to innovate. And innovating in the way the company delivered value to customers was the key.

T-Mobile's customer-first moves have disrupted the entire American telecom industry. But the lesson here is not that you must disrupt your industry to succeed.

It is that, to gain a sustainable edge, you must seek new ways to deliver value to consumers. And like T-Mobile, you cannot rest on your laurels; once you have created value for customers, you must build on that value, creating a consistent reputation for giving customers what they feel entitled to—or what they *will* feel entitled to once they get used to it.

Participants in our focus groups have continually cited companies that are doing just that.

They mentioned Zappos, the first online retailer to offer free shipping on both deliveries and returns.[5] Zappos has even extended free returns to a period of a full year after the original purchase, which puts people's minds at ease so that they can order shoes in various sizes and keep them only if they fit well.

They also mentioned USAA, the insurer and financial services company that focuses on military families. USAA frequently leads national customer experience rankings; it was one of the

To gain a sustainable edge, you must seek new ways to **DELIVER VALUE** to consumers.

top three banks for customer experience in the 2017 Temkin Experience Ratings.[6] It was the first bank to offer the ability to deposit a check by taking a picture on a mobile phone, an innovation that spread to become standard throughout the banking industry. USAA continues to create innovations focused on the specific needs of military families, like help with buying and selling homes for families that must frequently relocate, making payments and account access easier for people stationed overseas, and even banking with Amazon's Alexa.[7] When the US government looked like it might be shutting down due to a political dispute in early 2018, USAA offered no-interest loans to military members during the shutdown.[8]

The entitled consumers in our survey are on the lookout for value like this. A competitive price—cited by 68%—is table stakes. They're also looking for features like free shipping and returns (50%) and the ability to return the product or cancel the service without penalty (43%).

> *"You want to be a valued customer, okay? You want to be valued; you don't want to just be another number."*
>
> **STUART,** sales manager, UK

For consumer-first marketers, this continual quest to deliver more value should be no surprise. A marketer who treats you like a friend is always to going to be looking for opportunities to give you a little bit more of the things you like best. (A loudmouthed boor, on the other hand, is a lot less likely to be sensitive to what those things are.)

Your search for unique ways that your company can add customer value could go in almost any direction. But to get your thinking started, we'll take the rest of this chapter to describe six possible angles you could take:

1. Enhance your product or service.
2. Reduce consumer effort.
3. Improve customer experience.
4. Solve the consumer's broader problem.
5. Align your company with your consumers' values.
6. Encourage random acts of kindness.

While these are not the only possible ways for you to add value, our hope is that after reading some of the examples in this chapter, you'll be inspired to find new ways to add value within your own company.

ENHANCE YOUR PRODUCT OR SERVICE

Your customers are paying you for whatever you provide: mobile phone service, banking, a seat on a plane, a new car, or home improvement products, for example. Unfortunately, they are paying your competitors for exactly the same thing. If you're a retailer, you feature mostly the same products as the other guys. If you're a car company, your minivan gets a parent and her kids to

The benefits you use to differentiate won't be on your basic product or service; they'll be ANCILLARY benefits.

the soccer game in pretty much the same way as the competitor's minivan. In mature markets, most companies have fought each other to a standstill, since they have the same supply chains, the same access to advertising, and the same basic processes and costs.

Unless your company is very unusual, this means that the benefits you can use to differentiate won't be on your basic product or service. They'll be ancillary benefits.

Several UK retailers have pursued this strategy for holiday promotions. For example, Boots allows you to get makeup in a customized palette of colors or to personalize Christmas gifts with engraving. Selfridge's has deployed a service called "Elfridges"—personal shoppers you can communicate with in the store or online. And knitting supply store Wool and the Gang emails personalized offers based on previous purchases as well as a downloadable holiday checklist.[9]

Or consider Carnival Cruises. When you go on a cruise, you expect the food to be great, the entertainment to be fun, and the experience to be relaxing. But you probably don't expect to get screamingly fast 1.5 gigabit-per-second Wi-Fi for an online experience on a Carribbean cruise ship that's probably better than what you have at home.[10]

> **Cut costs that aren't monetary: the cost of the consumer's TIME and EFFORT.**

Ideally, these benefits create a sense of "wow!" Engraved Christmas gifts at Boots and gamer-level Wi-Fi on a ship are not what people expect. But in the age of entitled consumers, they surprise and delight consumers and help you stand out from your competitors. That's why a T-Mobile-type attitude of "what can we do for them next" is the key to long-term customer loyalty.

REDUCE CONSUMER EFFORT

Just as you can improve value by making your product or service better, you can also improve it by reducing cost. But driving prices lower is a challenging strategy; it reduces profits, it's easy for competitors to match, and it generally works only for the suppliers with the largest scale or the lowest quality. So you're better off cutting costs that aren't monetary—the cost of *time and effort.*

Affluent consumers particularly appreciate saving time and effort since they value their own time very highly. And for younger consumers—Millennials and Generation Z—wasting time with products that aren't optimized for their needs just won't fly. The entitled consumer wants your product to be easy and will go elsewhere if somebody else's is easier. In our surveys, 66% of consumers (and 75% of Fully Entitled consumers) agreed with the statement "When I encounter a new technology, site, or app, I can usually figure it out quickly." So make it easy, or you'll disappoint them.

With smartphones in the hands of nearly every consumer, mobile applications may be the most powerful way to reduce time and effort (see sidebar). And they create an ongoing competition to create easier ways to do business. When Starbucks introduced skip-the-line mobile ordering, Dunkin' Donuts was forced to follow suit. USAA forced a whole banking industry into mobile check deposit. E-Trade made mobile stock trading easy and, eventually, standard. Progressive Insurance automated competitive insurance quotes. Withings (now Nokia Health) made a scale that connected with your fitness app. Clorox made an app that tells you how to get stains out. Walgreens makes it effortless to turn your digital photos into calendars or key-

> For young consumers, wasting time with products that aren't **OPTIMIZED** for their needs just won't fly.

chains. Krispy Kreme even figured out how to send alerts when hot doughnuts have just come out of the oven in the closest store.

For the marketer, understanding the friction points in your customer's experience is the key to improving these time-and-effort challenges.

Mobile demands a focus on moments

What's your mobile strategy?

From our experience, this may be the wrong question. The consumer-first marketer should instead ask the question: What are the key moments in my customer's experience, and how can mobile ease interactions in those moments?[11]

To get started on mobile thinking, conduct an audit of mobile moments. If you're an airline, those moments might be when the customer books a reservation, reserves a seat, checks in, or arrives at the gate and boards the plane. If you're a retail store, your customer's moments might include selecting items to buy, requesting shipping, receiving a package, returning it, or interacting with an employee in the retail store. For each moment, consider the customer's goal, her history, and her context—use all available information to deliver a quick and easy interaction that solves the customer's problem in that moment.

The real challenge in mobile design goes deeper than what buttons you tap on a screen. Mobile applications must get instant access to customer information from corporate systems that were never designed to connect this quickly: CRM systems, reservation systems, and inventory systems, for example. Reengineering these systems for mobile moments are what can make mobile applications so challenging and expensive.

If you have service or retail staff that work with customers, remember that those staff have mobile moments of their own. (We saw this in Sophia's story in chapter 3, when the sales associate used a tablet to recall what Sophia was looking for and provided suggestions that matched her unique sense of style.)

For example, Trane, which installs residential air-conditioning systems, equipped its service staff with tablets that not only included all the necessary customer information but delivered animations demonstrating how air-conditioning options at different price points would function for the consumer. (Once the workers were armed with these tablets, their likelihood of closing a sale after a home visit went from 35% to 65%.) And, as we've mentioned, Delta Air Lines flight attendants use mobile devices to keep track of the needs and profiles of individual flyers while serving them in the air.

But regardless of whether your mobile efforts focus on employee or customer apps, text messages, push notifications, or even connected devices like Alexa or the Nest Thermostat, the strategic approach is the same: focus on the moments where your data can help a customer solve a problem, and then engineer your systems to make that interaction as quick and easy as possible.

IMPROVE CUSTOMER EXPERIENCE

When you take your kids to an amusement park, you expect to spend a lot of time throughout the day waiting in line. When you order room service at a hotel, you expect to pay exorbitant service and delivery fees. When your cable or satellite stops working, you expect to waste time and energy on the phone, sometimes waiting

You don't have to disrupt an industry to improve your customer's experience in ways that **EXCEED** expectations.

days to get it working again. When an airline delays a flight, you expect to hear an excuse you only half-believe accompanied by shrugged shoulders.

Maybe you shouldn't. Some companies are introducing ways of doing business that surprise you, creating a differentiated, startlingly easy, and enjoyable level of service. In some cases, these companies have disrupted whole industries: consider how much easier Uber is than a taxi, how Airbnb delivers more choices at cheaper prices than hotels, or how Netflix allows you to stream premium entertainment content on your own schedule.

But you don't have to disrupt an industry to improve your customer's experience in ways that exceed expectations. It might be the pleasant surprise of a convenient alert letting you know at which baggage carousel your luggage will appear the moment your flight lands. You might appreciate a text from your utility company that explains that it is working on an outage and predicts when you'll get the power back. You might appreciate when your storage company lets you know of potential storm damage. Or you might like a single customer service rep owning your case until it is resolved, providing you with his contact details, and sharing a timeline of when and how the problem will be solved.

> *"If something is good quality and I've had a good experience, I'll pay for that, whether it be clothes, a watch, whatever."*
>
> **STUART,** sales manager, UK

Consumers' preconceived expectations about a product or service heavily influence their perception of value. That expectation is based on our experience within a given industry; we put up with shoddy service from our telecom and cable companies because we are used to it, and competitors offered an experience that was no better. But consumers now tell us that their expectations of companies in all industries are rising based on their experiences in other industries—it's the transference of entitlement again, and regardless of what industry you work in, it's now your problem. The transference of entitlement means that every company is competing on an experience baseline set by Amazon, Disney, and USAA. And it means that just because you've always had to wait on hold to speak to your cable company doesn't mean that you will be willing to accept it anymore.

When we asked consumers in our survey about how they react when a product or service doesn't meet their expectations, more than a third (34% of all consumers, and 36% of Fully Entitled consumers) told us that they would never buy from the company again. Many will also tell their friends and family about their negative experience (37% of all consumers and 40% of Fully Entitled consumers) and some—enough to cause trouble—will post or share about their negative experience on social media (12% of all consumers and 17% of Fully Entitled consumers). Even in an industry with annoying problems and lagging customer experience, entitled customers expect better. Give it to them, and they'll pick you over the competition.

Consumers' preconceived expectations about a product or service **HEAVILY** influence their perception of value.

In the past twelve months, all three of us authors have experienced companies that exceeded expectations. We got five thousand bonus miles and a nice note when a flight was delayed due to mechanical problems. We saw an outdoor gear manufacturer replace a worn-out product three years after we bought it. We got a hotel upgrade because we arrived just plain exhausted. And as a result, we have begun to expect other companies to provide compensation when things go wrong, to stand by the quality of their product over its lifetime, or to just do something nice for no reason every once in a while (see sidebar).

Marketers hoping to create an experience that exceeds expectations must start by asking the implicit, often forbidden question: "Why does it have to be this way?" (Think about T-Mobile's marketers asking, "Why do customers need to be locked into contracts?" and "Why should people have to pay extra for service when they travel?")

Often, these solutions are digital. For example, Ikea asked the question, "Why can't customers see how that piece of furniture will look in their homes?" Taking the furniture home, assembling it, and then bringing it back if it doesn't look quite right was clearly impractical. Ikea figured out a better solution: an augmented reality app.[12] You find the furniture in the catalog, scan it with the app, and then point your tablet or smartphone at the spot in the room where you want to put it. A little digital dragging and zooming—far easier than dragging around actual furniture—and you can get an idea of how the couch or table will look and what color matches best.

One in three consumers say they'd NEVER buy from a company again if it fails to meet their expectations.

Then there's GiffGaff, a new kind of mobile operator in the UK. GiffGaff asked the question, "Why can't consumers design their own mobile plans?" Its online community allows consumers to propose and comment on new ways of structuring mobile plans and pricing. To make the pricing work, the company doesn't require you to buy phones from GiffGaff; you instead purchase a SIM card, which you can slide into a phone you get elsewhere. And it doesn't maintain a call center for technical support; you get answers from other customers on the highly active customer community. Customer satisfaction is 90%.[13]

To exceed expectations, ask the implicit, often forbidden question: "WHY does it have to be this way?"

Like the Carnival Cruises with its fast Wi-Fi, these companies make doing business with them easier in unexpected ways. What are the pain points for your customers, and how could you provide an unexpectedly better experience by improving them?

Customer experience is more than a buzzword

Marketers love to talk about "customer experience" as if it were a well-understood concept. But in the past ten years or so, customer experience (CX) has grown from a squishy idea into a full-fledged business discipline.

In Outside In: The Power of Putting Customers at the Center of Your Business, *Harley Manning and Kerry Bodine define CX simply as "how your customers perceive their interactions with your business."[14] A description this broad stretches across all sorts of customer interactions, from becoming interested in your company to purchases to using your products and services and requesting tech support. For any given interaction, the experience may range from basic (it met customers' needs) to easy (they didn't have to work at it) to enjoyable (they actually felt good about it). Your job as a consumer-first marketer is to find ways to create ease and enjoyment in as many interactions as possible.*

A disciplined approach to CX requires research on where your customers' pain points are—and what about your business is holding them back—and how intelligently designed processes can improve those problems. You'll need to learn to measure CX on an ongoing basis, improve your culture so that it is more experience-focused, and align the company strategy around customer experience.

It's no coincidence that the leaders in CX surveys are companies like USAA, FedEx, Southwest Airlines, and the UK's Virgin Media. These companies have a commitment from the top to put strategies, process designs, and measurement in place to make an overall effort to build CX improvement into the way the company does business. At Safelite AutoGlass, for example, local auto-glass replacement shops compete on customer experience scores, and the company shares and recognizes those that are outstanding. Cleveland Clinic has a customer experience executive in the C-suite who has the companywide responsibility to improve the experience of patients.

A consumer-first approach has the potential to dramatically improve customer experience by making marketing more relevant and less annoying and by using the customer's own information to customize interactions and make them more efficient. This is why consumer-first marketing and a focus on customer experience typically go hand in hand.

SOLVE THE CONSUMER'S BROADER PROBLEM

Skiing is expensive. All that equipment costs a lot. But great equipment—like boots that fit perfectly—makes the experience much better. Comfortable, quality, well-fitted ski boots can make the difference between giving up and loving the sport.

The problem is the cost, especially if you have children. Their little feet don't tend to stay the same size from season to season, and buying new boots every year vastly inflates your vacation budget.

Consider the consumer's **ENTIRE CHALLENGE,** not just the part associated with one transaction, to create reciprocal value for a lasting relationship.

Surefoot, a retailer of custom-fitted boots that has now grown from a tiny, closet-size location in Park City, Utah, to two dozen locations throughout North America and Europe, set out to solve this problem. It had already sold half a million custom-fitted boot liners when it developed its Growing Pains program.[15] When a kid outgrows the boots, the parents get a 50% discount on each pair of boots and a free replacement of the custom insoles that make the fit so good, provided they return the old boots within two years. You might think Surefoot leaves a lot of potential revenue on the slopes, but it's creating a consistent stream of repeat business and a maturing set of customers who will be forever loyal.

Surefoot's insight is to consider not just the consumer's immediate problem—finding boots that fit well—but the larger problem: finding ski equipment that remains comfortable and safe for growing children. This approach—considering the consumer's entire challenge, not just the part associated with one transaction—is one way to create reciprocal value for a lasting relationship. Here are some other examples:

"Airbnb and Booking.com are both helpful in the way that they prepare you for your stay and wherever you're going. They [email] you sightseeing tips, transport tips, all sorts of tips that you really need as a traveler."

SARAH, psychologist, Germany

- **Darn Tough socks have a lifetime guarantee without strings or conditions.** You could walk the whole Appalachian trail in a pair and, if they then wear out, return them to the company for a new pair.[16] Although the official policy requires an owner to return them to the company, many independent gear stores will replace them on the spot, and we have even heard of through-hikers exchanging socks in local stores midtrail.

- **Sephora offers a free Beauty TIP workshop to women who visit its store.** But while many beauty retailers will help you try new products, Sephora keeps a record of all the products you try and prints it out for you take with you so you can duplicate the look you've created in your bathroom or at your vanity table. If you can't get to a store, the Sephora to Go app will let you try out products that match your skin tone; then you can place orders to have them delivered to your home.[17]

- **Tesla has integrated service directly into the car experience.** Many Tesla upgrades happen with over-the-air electronic updates to the car's software and interface, delivering new capabilities without the need for a trip to the dealership. The company claims that 90% of all service-related issues can be diagnosed without bringing the car in for service; if a diagnostic detects a problem, the service center can often correct it with a simple software update.[18] And Tesla says the optimized workflow in its service centers makes the process of getting your car fixed four times as fast as a typical repair facility.

In each of these cases, the company has considered the consumer's broader problem—holey socks, looking great, keeping cars running—and determined a way to solve that problem by expanding the value proposition. These kinds of improvements create the edge that keeps customers loyal.

ALIGN YOUR COMPANY WITH YOUR CONSUMERS' VALUES

Values matter to entitled consumers: 34% of Fully Entitled consumers told us that they "only shop from places that support the same causes that I do." For some consumers, especially Millennials and Generation Z, understanding how the companies that they patronize operate is important, and aligning with their values is paramount.

According to Forrester, the proportion of US online adults who consider company values when making a purchase decision has risen from 43% in 2015 to 52% in 2017.[19] One in five US online adults strive to prioritize company values over factors like price and convenience, especially in categories like food and grocery, household products, and electronics. In its 2017 report "Align With Consumers' Values To Win Their Hearts And Wallets," Forrester recommends focusing on values that have relevance and resonance for your consumer base, incorporating those values throughout your company, and then creating tangible evidence of your commitment to those values.[20] This type of strategic thinking explains, for example, why, shortly after two African American men were arrested simply for waiting for a meeting in a Starbucks, the coffee company shuttered all of its stores for one day to focus on training its entire workforce on issues of race and tolerance.

One pioneering values-focused brand is TOMS Shoes, the creator of the "buy one, give one" model of helping the less fortunate. Customers that bought a pair of TOMS could feel good about not only their purchase for themselves but in knowing that a second pair would be donated to someone who couldn't afford proper shoes. After receiving negative feedback that its model was hurting small local businesses in the countries where it operated, TOMS adapted its approach and began to manufacture shoes in Haiti, employing local workers and using local materials with the hope of creating a sustainable Haitian industry.[21]

Since then, scores of other companies have pursued the buy-one-give-one model with products ranging from backpacks (Bixbee and State) to chewing gum (Project 7), eyeglasses (Warby Parker and Toms), groceries (Thrive Market), and medical scrubs (Figs). In each case, customers get added value from knowing that they provided a product that will help those in greater need. The alignment of values provides a form of self-actualization and affiliation to the buyer.

Buy-one-give-one is certainly not the only model of values alignment as a source of reciprocal value for customers. Novo Nordisk, a Danish pharmaceutical company, supplies around half of the world's insulin, often at reduced prices in developing countries.[22] Natura, a Brazilian cosmetics company, helps preserve the Amazon rainforest by creating greater demand for living-forest products such as seeds and nuts. Newman's Own, the food company, donates 100% of its profits—more than $500 million to date—to educational and charitable organizations.[23]

Not all values alignment is purely charitable. Some of it looks more like activism. When Coup, a new cocktail bar in New York, promised in April 2017 to donate all of its profits to charities whose missions might be affected by the Trump administration in the United States, it joined the ranks of companies using their brand to promote specific causes. Sleeping Giant, an anonymous watchdog organization, publicly alerts brands when their advertising appears on extremist media websites (sometimes without the brand's knowledge) and encourages them to blacklist the websites in question.

Starwood Hotels gives customers the option to "Make a Green Choice" while staying at their hotels. The program gives customers 500 Starwoods loyalty points to guests that opt out of housekeeping services for the duration of their stay. It frees up staff from cleaning the room, conserves water and energy by reducing the amount of bed linen and towels that are washed daily, and rewards the customer for participating. In our focus group in Germany, several participants said that they prefer to use the search engine Ecosia, which has used its profits to plant more than 25 million trees.[24]

Values alignment can have repercussions as well, as Delta Air Lines found out when it cancelled a discount for National Rifle Association members going to the organization's national convention. In retaliation, conservatives in the Georgia state legislature cancelled a fuel tax break planned for Delta's major hub airport in Atlanta.

But when it comes to perceived value, companies that identify the causes their customers believe in and that find creative and appropriate ways to support those causes will create yet another way to differentiate themselves in the consumer's mind.

ENCOURAGE RANDOM ACTS OF KINDNESS

On March 16, 2018, Aer Lingus, the Irish national airline, gave every passenger on a flight from Dublin to London a free Irish rugby jersey. This wasn't just an early St. Patrick's Day surprise. The next day, Ireland played England and won the rugby grand slam for only the third time in the nation's history. Passengers were asked to "remain in their Ireland jerseys for the duration of the weekend." Within minutes, hundreds of thousands of people were talking about the gesture and raising pints of Guinness to Aer Lingus on Facebook, Twitter, and Instagram.

Obviously, random acts of kindness don't scale. Or do they? Companies that encourage their employees to identify and pursue these opportunities for small, sympathetic (and typically, low-cost) gestures will see them spread throughout their service organizations. And these efforts pay off not only for the individual customer who benefits but for the company as well when thousands of others may hear about it as the news spreads on social media.

Hotels are a great example. I (Josh) once had a frustrating and disappointing experience with a Hyatt hotel in Philadelphia and wrote about it on social media. A month later, when I'd pretty much forgotten what had happened, I checked into a Hyatt in Seattle and unexpectedly got upgraded to a suite; when I arrived in the room, there was plate of cheese and fruit and a nice bottle of wine, along with a note from the manager of the Hyatt that had disappointed me in Philadelphia. I made sure to write a blog post about how the company had taken the extra effort to remember my issue, look up my next reservation, and make up for the trouble it had caused me. Hyatt CEO Mark Hoplamazian encourages these random acts of generosity—like picking up a random customer's bar tab—as a sign of the hospitality the brand is trying to deliver.[25]

Identify the CAUSES that your customers believe in, and find creative and appropriate ways to support those causes to create a source of differentiation.

Employees at Disney theme parks are so committed to a customer-focused way to perform that the company calls them "cast members." Naturally, you'd expect the people whose job it is to dress as Winnie the Pooh or Elsa to shower kind attention on the park's young visitors. But the spirit extends beyond the staff dressed as characters. One security guard at the park has made it his practice to carry an autograph book and ask for autographs from little girls who arrive dressed as princesses. As Barbara Bunchuk, one young girl's grandmother, wrote, her granddaughter Alli "was very much into the princesses and had to wear her princess dress...Upon entering the Magic Kingdom, one of the security guards said to Alli, 'Excuse me, Princess, can I have your autograph?' I could see that the book was filled with children's scribbles as the guard asked the same question of many little Princesses. Alli could not get over the fact that the guard thought she was a real princess."[26] Her photos of the event spread widely on Pinterest, Tumblr, and Reddit.

Employees' acts of kindness pay off when **THOUSANDS** of others hear about them on social media posts.

At the UK cable operator Virgin Media, a customer service rep who heard a customer mention that he had new grandchildren mailed a picture frame with a handwritten note. At Rackspace, a supplier of cloud Internet services, a rep engaged in a marathon troubleshooting session with a client overheard the client say to colleagues how hungry he was and ordered a pizza delivered to his office.[27] And at the online shoe retailer Zappos, random acts of kindness are part of the culture: "Deliver WOW through service." and "Be Adventurous, Creative, and Open-Minded" are written right in the company's core values.[28] That's wh y when a customer named Zaz Lamarr explained that she had meant to return some shoes but had been preoccupied by the death of her mother, Zappos sent a huge bouquet of flowers.[29]

These acts are remarkable. So people remark on them. You can bet that the customers who received these random acts of kindness will stay loyal. But they'll also become advocates, helping these companies to win over their friends and everyone else who hears about these random acts on social media channels.

CONCENTRATE ON MOMENTS—AND USE DATA TO DELIVER VALUE

Google has a name for the moments when consumers turn to their devices to take action on whatever they need or want right then: "micro-moments."[30] Google breaks down the micro-moments into four distinct categories: I want to know, I want to go, I want to buy, and I want to do. Each of these micro-moments is loaded with intent, context, and intimacy. For marketers, they are loaded with opportunity to deliver value. If you look back at all the examples of value we've included in this chapter, they tend to connect with customers at a specific micro-moment: the moment a little girl dressed as a princess arrives at a Disney park, the moment the USAA banking customer wants to deposit a check, or the moment the Tesla owner realizes her car has new capabilities and that she didn't have to do anything to make that happen.

> **Each of a consumer's micro-moments is LOADED with the opportunity to deliver value.**

But as fascinating as all the examples of ways to add value in this chapter are, they tend to be brand-wide examples. That means they're often the same for every customer. And that means they can be much, much better with an added dose of personalization.

To be as successful as possible, these new sources of value need to become visible at the perfect moment—the moment when you need to make sure a check won't bounce, or when your flight just got cancelled, or when you're stuck in traffic and running late. Value has a maximum impact when it is personal. That's because it won't be exactly the same for every customer—it will be maximally *relevant* for every customer.

In the next chapter, we'll show you just how to do that.

THE CONSUMER-FIRST MARKETER'S TO-DO LIST

These are your to-dos to improve the way your company delivers reciprocal value:

- ☐ Look at your customer's broader problem, and work on ways to solve that.
- ☐ To gain a sustainable edge, seek new ways to deliver value to your consumers.
- ☐ Focus on ancillary benefits that you can add to enhance your product experience.
- ☐ Align your company's values with your consumer's.
- ☐ Find ways to encourage random acts of kindness as part of your company's culture.
- ☐ Look for ways to reduce the effort your consumer must make to use your products.

ALERT
ALERT
ALERT
Having trouble sleeping? $5 off Night-time Sleep-Aid Liquidcaps
Close
View
TOM FISH BURNE
© marketoonist.com

Chapter 7

RELEVANCE STRENGTHENS RELATIONSHIPS

Thomas Rubens[1] loves art house movies. And he's especially fond of Woody Allen films. One day he gets an email from Kinepolis, a cinema chain operating throughout several European countries, promoting a Hollywood romantic comedy. Normally, you'd expect him to send that email right to the trash, possibly even to unsubscribe from Kinepolis' emails. But he clicks on it and reads about the big-budget rom-com. Renée Zellweger is starring, and Rubens thinks it sounds like it might be fun. He takes his wife to see it that weekend—and doesn't particularly notice the fact that the email from Kinepolis prompted a successful date night with his wife.

How did that happen? Kinepolis, at least as it relates to movies, knows its customers better than they know themselves. While Rubens goes to a lot of art house movies and identifies himself as an art house movie lover, Kinepolis knows that his interests aren't limited to art house. How? His actions give him away. He provides Kinepolis with nuggets of insight every time he opens an email, taps the Kinepolis app, updates his wish list on the Kinepolis site, goes to a movie, or completes a survey. Kinepolis, in turn, builds a profile of Rubens that combines his declared preferences with a shadow profile based on his observed behavior and activity.

Kinepolis uses these rich consumer profiles to inform every interaction that it has with its customers. Kinepolis seeks to limit its communication only to content that is most relevant to each individual consumer. For example, in the Belgian market, Kinepolis emails an average of 7% of its database in any given mailing. It starts from the point of view of the consumer, employing an approach it calls "marketing as a service." The company doesn't want to send the email to the other 93% of its customers because, at any given moment, it doesn't have a message good enough to adequately be of service to them.

The idea of marketing as a service is the brainchild of Stefaan Claes, the international CRM and digital marketing director for Kinepolis. Stefaan's mantra of marketing as a service is all about being as selective as possible. In his words, it is about "limiting communications and interactions to those that deliver value and a service to the consumer."

Does it work? Consider that as of 2018, Kinepolis has grown to operate 94 theater locations, up from 23 in 2013.

Stefaan talks about his and Kinepolis' dedication to marketing as a service in almost religious terms. "When we started on this journey, I was an evangelist," he told us. "Today, six or seven years later, there are a lot of believers. To understand whether what we do has an impact, we look at everything from the open rates of our messages to our ticket sales. Every two years, we survey our customers and ask about our communication. When we ask whether the films we recommend are what they want to see, 65% to 70% say we're doing it 'good' to 'perfect,'" Stefaan explains.

If a communication is not relevant, it is irrelevant. Friends don't send **IRRELEVANT** messages; neither should marketers.

Getting consumer-first marketing right requires a mind shift, as Stefaan demonstrates. And that mind shift needs to be supported by a change in attitude.

RELEVANCE IS CRUCIAL TO RELATIONSHIPS

If you don't want your marketing to be perceived as an overload of messages, relevance is the key. If a communication is not relevant, it is irrelevant. And friends don't send irrelevant messages. That's what loudmouthed boors do.

If your marketers are sending a series of irrelevant messages, the consumer will see your company as irrelevant. Entitled consumers expect marketers to contact them only with information that's just what they are looking for, at the moment they are looking for it. From the marketer's perspective, those messages are the ones most likely to enrich and deepen your relationship with customers, just as Kinepolis is deepening its relationship with consumers like Thomas.

We'd like to you to get to a point where your customers perceive you as helpful, your messages as useful, and your company as relevant to what they want.

The **ATTENTION** of your consumer is the most valuable asset you have.

To do that, you must think differently about your customers. You must follow this principle:

The attention of your consumer is the most valuable asset you have.

What will you do with that attention?

Will you extend and deepen it by sending relevant messages that the consumer finds useful?

Or will you use it up with irrelevant messages that will be perceived as spam—and ruin your brand and relationship in the process?

In this chapter, we'll describe four ways to increase your relevance—and show how some successful marketers have turned them into strategies that pay off in long-term relationships:

- Use all relevant information to build profiles.
- Use what you know to make things easier for the consumer.
- Use your knowledge to send the most relevant possible message.
- If you don't have something useful to say, don't say anything.

USE ALL RELEVANT INFORMATION TO BUILD PROFILES

As we described in chapter 4, data is the fuel that makes consumer-first marketing work. Remember Lode Van Laere at the Belgian retailer JBC, who used the company's knowledge of consumers' shopping habits to customize the right offer at the right moment? Lode knew just what to put in each message—the most relevant information to create value for the customer. That's the attitude that all marketers must take.

You can gather information like that from your relationship with the customer. You can get it from third parties like Acxiom, Callcredit, or Oracle, which collect data on consumers such as their age, the car they own, how many children they have, and their credit score. Or you can ask people for information to help you create more relevant messages.

But the key is to gather information that will be useful for creating relevance in your messages, not just a sprawling dossier of everything you can find. For that reason, we recommend following a few rules of thumb:

1. **Don't ask for more information than you'll use.** As we described in chapter 4, collecting data you don't need wastes the consumer's time and raises her expectation that you'll use the information. Entitled consumers are impatient, so ask as few questions as you can about the topics most likely to create relevance in future communications. Stefaan at Kinepolis has every reason to know if you'd be interested in attending movie premieres, but he has no reason to ask what your favorite beer is or the size of your mortgage.

2. **Only ask for what you don't know (or can't figure out).** Trial lawyers follow a simple principle in cross-examinations: never ask a question if you don't already know what the answer will be. As a marketer, you must take the diametrically opposite approach: *only* ask a question if you don't already know the answer. If you can make a reasonable guess at the answer, then asking the consumer is just redundant overhead (you know, like when

you call customer service and they keep asking for your account number again and again). Entitled consumers will respect you—and value the relationship more—if you take advantage of everything you know to serve them better, rather than pestering them for information you should already know.

3. **Be clear why you're asking.** If you need my date of birth, I'll provide it. But if you ask for it and I don't understand why you need it, I'm more likely to abandon our exchange altogether. JBC's request for the birthdays of a customer's children makes sense, because the company creates a custom offer on the kids' birthdays. But asking for mom's social security number would probably make her ask, "Why do you want to know?" In our surveys, 29% of Fully Entitled consumers said they had much higher expectations of service and/or relevance when a company was gathering their data. We'll talk in more detail about the imperative to be transparent about data you're collecting in the next chapter.

4. **Focus on what's most immediately important.** You don't have to get all the information at once. Capture what's most important and employ a strategy of "progressive profiling" to enhance the information over time. Remember, this is a relationship. As it gets more comfortable, your customers will reveal more information over time.

Gather information that will be useful for creating RELEVANCE in your messages, not just a sprawling dossier of everything you can find.

And remember, there's no point in asking about what you can hear and observe instead. For example, consumers might demonstrate their preference for certain content, product lines, or offers based on where they spend their time on your website. (Remember Sophia's preference for clothing with rock-and-roll logos?) Or they might share their opinion with friends and family in social media. When returning an item, even the most entitled consumer is usually willing to provide a reason. By listening to the consumer's signals, marketers can learn a great deal about her interests, motivations, and implicit preferences. You can—and should—harness and add these to a consumer's profile; think about Thomas Rubens' stated preferences for art house and Woody Allen movies and his behavioral proclivity toward Zellweger rom-coms. By both asking and listening, marketers can build a far more accurate picture of the consumer than employing either one technique on its own would allow.

There's NO POINT in asking consumers for information that you can hear and observe instead.

Marketers can also listen for more than implicit preferences—they can collect data from social networks, as we described in chapter 4. Social listening platforms, such as Synthesio, Brandwatch, Sprinklr, and NetBase, and newer AI solutions, like SentiSum, enable marketers to capture consumer sentiment and interest, particularly across social media. These solutions give firms the opportunity to provide customer service in response to consumer concerns, help measure brand health and campaign success, and surface product ideas by listening to unmet consumer needs. But don't limit how you listen, learn, and react to the social channel. Marry that information with the consumer's profile to inform all future interactions regardless of where the engagement takes place.

USE WHAT YOU KNOW TO MAKE THINGS EASIER FOR THE CUSTOMER

If you can make it easier for customers to do business with you, you'll get more business. This is the main value of the profile you've gathered: to make it easy to do business with you.

> *"Google knows my preferences; therefore, I get offers that will match my preferences, and that's not a bad thing. I find it quite helpful if Google just recommends a couple of things and I can still go through the decision process."*
>
> **SARAH,** psychologist, Germany

Take Allstate home insurance as an example. Normally, to get a quote for home insurance, the customer must fill out at least twenty different fields in a form. This is an arduous task.

To ease that burden, Ben Gaddis, president of the T3 agency in Austin, worked with Allstate to create the experience they refer to as "GoodHome," which collects content from eight different data sources. When you visit the site, it attempts to detect your address and asks you to confirm. It then fills in the blanks. It uses Google Street View to show a photo and to suggest information about the home, like the number of bedrooms, the number of bathrooms, the date it was built, the type of construction, and, of course, its estimated value. All this information is easily accessible to Allstate, but insurers have historically asked their customers to provide it by filling out forms. After that, Allstate's GoodHome page shares statistics from your neighborhood about risks like fire, theft, and water or snow damage, along with ways to economize on energy costs. Consumers who visit the site are three-and-a-half times more likely to request a quote than they were when visiting the plain old "get me a quote" site that Allstate used to have. As Ben told us, "This makes Allstate's interactions with customers more personal—and to succeed, interactions have to be not just targeted but truly personal."

If you can make it EASIER for customers to do business with you, you'll get more business.

Ben's agency T3 also worked on an application for office managers from Staples. By observing office managers in small businesses, Staples was able to get a good idea of the office manager's day—a day typically filled with people emailing, swinging by the desk, or just shouting about things they need, like dry-erase markers and coffee supplies. Staples developed a smart speaker, powered by IBM's Watson, that can respond to requests like, "I need a box of black Sharpies and a case of the paper I ordered last week" and add appropriate items to an online shopping cart. The office manager can also forward random email requests from coworkers to the application, which then interprets them and adds them to the cart. On the day the office manager places the office supplies order—say, Friday—she verifies the items in the cart based on all the requests that came in through emails, voice, and every other channel. If she's satisfied, she presses one button to place the order.

This Staples smart ordering system is now in 1,000 businesses that have high order frequencies from Staples. And in those locations, customer satisfaction with Staples is much higher. It's the real-life embodiment of the "Easy" button featured in Staples ads in the US.

As Ben describes it, "One of the challenges we face with entitled consumers is, they don't want tech. They want a better experience." That what T3 built for Staples' customers. "It's a game-changing experience. The office admin wants easier ordering. If we make that easy, Staples makes more money. It's a full suite of solutions for an entire office with one-day shipping [because Staples is local]; even Amazon can't do that."

The Fully Entitled consumers we surveyed were all over the "make it easy" idea; as we showed in chapter 5, 71% would be happy if an airline popped up the boarding pass as soon as they got to the airport, 65% would like to be able to check into a hotel room without visiting the front desk, and 58% would like it if their insurance company tracked their driving behavior and adjusted their premiums accordingly.

All of these types of applications take data. Consumers implicitly know that. And they're generally fine with it, as long as you're using the data to improve their experience.

USE YOUR KNOWLEDGE TO SEND THE MOST RELEVANT POSSIBLE MESSAGE

To maximize relevance, it's not enough to send the right offer. The right message—which might or might not be an offer—is only the right message *at the right moment*.

In chapter 4, we explained Heraclitus' explanation of how a man could never step in the same river twice. In the same way, a profile—like the man in Heraclitus' example—may be the same, but the situation is different. To decide what to say—or, perhaps, to say nothing—you must know the context of the person with whom you are communicating. The question is not, "What am I going to tell him." It is, "Should I tell him something *right now*?"

"With apps, it is convenient, it's more personalized than it used to be. They're showing you stuff that's more relevant. It used to be, you just felt like you were being spammed constantly online. At least it's a little bit more target-driven now. I love it. It's amazing."

JESS, admin, UK

That's what Esther Poulsen of the Raare Solutions agency did for the CRM and experiential marketing teams at one manufacturer of performance cars.

The carmaker runs a series of driving events in the United States, including teen driving schools, special test-driving events, and VIP experiences. These events are popular. In fact, they're too popular; they tend to fill up with customers who love to drive new cars but who might not actually be in the market to buy one.

So Esther and her team collaborated with the carmaker to create a comprehensive, standardized system to keep track of all the company's drivers and prospects. She knows who is on their fifth lease and gets a new car every three years—and who just bought their first vehicle from this brand last year. And she knows which customers have kids who are about to become teenagers.

As a result, the car manufacturer can customize the way the invitations go out. The frequent, repeat buyers who are just about ready for a new lease get the first set of VIP invitations. The families get teen driving invitations. The rest receive a general event invitation. These messages go out through multiple channels: direct mail, banner ads, and emails.

Once those invitations go out, if there are spaces left, then messages go out to people who are less likely to be hot prospects, eventually trickling down to those who just bought or leased a car recently or are less qualified leads.

The message timing is completely optimized as well, going out at the time of day and day of week a customer is most likely to respond.

And it's working. The carmaker ramped up the messages as they became more effective. Then it then ramped them down a bit starting in 2015 to cut back on messaging overload. But even as the number of messages has come down, sales have gone up. That's strong evidence that the new strategy is working.

Sophisticated, customized messaging strategies like this work in retail as well. Jan Biłyk, the CEO of the Polish marketing agency Laurens Coster, showed us some vivid examples. He created marketing programs for two of Poland's biggest retailers: the leading bookstore in Poland (Empik) and one of the biggest drugstore chains. In both cases, the key element was the loyalty cards that the chains' customers had gotten in the habit of using as they shopped.

At Empik, Jan made sure that if a customer bought a book, she'd get a recommendation a week or two later for additional books by the same author, about the same topic, or in the same genre—leveraging historical data from the relationship, as we recommended in chapter 4. The program extended to CDs, DVDs, and games as well. Empik carried 2 million titles, not all of which would be in stock at any given moment. So the bookstore would also send messages based on events in the store's inventory, such as when a relevant title came back in stock or if the price of a book had changed.

Empik customizes email based on events in the world, too. If a famous person has just died, received a Nobel prize, or appeared locally in a concert or on TV, products related to that person were more likely to appear in the email. Even then, the mix of products in any email would depend not just on what was happening in Poland and what just went on sale in the store but also on what would appeal to that specific customer.

The result was a program that identified five to ten unique products and emailed the customers—over two million of them—every two weeks. Each email fit the customer's unique cultural interests, so the customers actually welcomed them. More importantly, *they actually opened them*. "When we mention the name of the product you have browsed or bought, in Empik, open rates are through the roof compared to a generic email or one just mentioning your name in subject line," Jan says.

The drugstores, of course, had a much more diverse set of products to sell. But Jan and his team continued to focus on relevance. "We don't want to exhaust people with too many promotions," Jan explains. So they sent emails or phone text messages when the relevant product for that customer—favorite toothpaste, hair gel, or box of bath salts—has a special price and only when they are sure the customer hasn't just bought a new bottle or box of it. They wait to be sure that the purchase was a little while ago and the customer might be running out.

These messages apply not only in the customer's email but also in the store. If you check out at the drugstore register and use your loyalty card—which two million Polish customers of this drugstore chain do—then the salesperson at the checkout gets a display prompt on her screen so she can make recommendations on other products you've bought in the past or might be interested in just at that moment.

Based on calculations for all the loyalty card holders, Jan estimates that marketing messages directed to them generate over 10% of total sales. And his agency also estimates that a customized message about products the customer is likely to be interested in *right now* is twice as effective as a generic message to the same customer.

A customized message about products the customer is likely to be interested in **RIGHT NOW** can be twice as effective as a generic message to the same customer.

Consumer surveys confirm Jan's intuitions. In a 2017 survey of over 1,000 consumers, customer data platform provider Segment found that 54% of people expect to receive a personalized discount from a retailer within 24 hours of identifying themselves, and 63% say receiving a discount within an hour of interacting with a brand will drive loyalty.[2]

IF YOU DON'T HAVE SOMETHING USEFUL TO SAY, DON'T SAY ANYTHING

Here's one more nugget from of insight from Jan Biłyk and his agency.

His agency knows when *not* to send messages.

If there is a fresh customer, she gets a maximum of three emails and one text message per week. (Poles are a lot more comfortable with marketing through text messages than Americans are, but, of course, their preferences vary.)

After that, the customer gets to decide. If she is tired of the communication and clicks to unsubscribe, the drugstore chain offers her the chance to choose to get messages less frequently instead. If the customer failed to open ten consecutive messages, the drugstore will stop sending for a month; then it will restart and see what happens.

On the other hand, if somebody reads every single email, the drugstore will ramp up the frequency and send more.

And based on the data from its loyalty cards, the store knows what is likely to convert. If a message is likely to generate a sale, the store will send it. If not, it just won't send it at all.

This strategy helps avoid generating the feeling of marketing overload that annoys so many customers, as we described in chapter 2.

This extremely high rate of relevance has counterintuitive consequences. By sending fewer messages—and only those that are most relevant—the drugstore ensures that customers have a positive feeling about the emails they are receiving. There have even been cases where, because the messages were so personalized, that people complained if a friend received a notification for a special that they didn't receive.

By sending **FEWER** messages—and only those that are most relevant—you ensure that customers have a positive feeling about the emails they are receiving.

When your customers are complaining about not getting enough marketing, you're in an excellent position.

RELEVANCE IS A DISCIPLINE

It's easy to send irrelevant messages based on your needs as a marketer. It's "spray and pray" all over again. And so many marketers have done this that the world is now polluted with irrelevant messages—it's what consumers expect of you.

Defy those expectations. Behave like a friend. Build a relationship. They'll be more likely to open your emails, respond to your text messages, interact with your ads, and take action on your website. Not only that, they'll be more likely to stick around and become loyal customers. They won't think of your marketing as marketing. And that's why it will be effective.

THE CONSUMER-FIRST MARKETER'S TO-DO LIST

These are your to-dos to improve the way your company delivers relevance:

- ☐ Collect all relevant information to build consumer profiles.
- ☐ Don't ask for information you don't know how to use or for information you can't figure out from other sources.
- ☐ Be transparent about why you're asking for information.
- ☐ Add information from social listening platforms.
- ☐ Use the information you've gathered to make things easier for customers.
- ☐ Send the most relevant possible messages at the moment they are most likely to be helpful.
- ☐ If you don't have anything useful to send, don't send a message at all.

UNITED
CANCELED
DOOMED
HOSED
SHAFTED
FUBAR
DEPARTURES
YOUR CALL IS VERY IMPORTANT TO US. PLEASE HOLD WHILE WE EVAPORATE ALL THE GOODWILL CREATED BY OUR EXPENSIVE ADVERTISING.
TOM FISHBURNE
© marketoonist.com

Chapter 8

RESPECTFUL EMPATHY PRESERVES RELATIONSHIPS

For some companies, it's a bad time for trust.

Take Uber. In the past few years, Uber and its executives have been accused of: bragging they would expose incriminating information about journalists who criticize them; maintaining a workplace culture steeped in sexual harassment; tracking people even after their Uber app was off; surreptitiously avoiding giving rides to law enforcement personnel; stealing secrets about self-driving cars from a sister company of Google; ordering and cancelling rides from competitors; failing to provide the full amount of promised compensation to drivers in New York

City; and making blackmail payments to hackers who had stolen information about over 57 million riders.

In April of 2018, a self-driving Uber vehicle in a pilot program in Arizona ran over and killed a woman. Uber's public statements were limited to this tweet: "Our hearts go out to the victim's family. We're fully cooperating with Tempe [Arizona] Police and local authorities as they investigate this incident."[1]

Over 30,000 people die on the American roads every year. Uber's autonomous cars killed a single person after thousands of miles of driving. Should we give Uber the benefit of the doubt on this one?

Based on Uber's past history, no. Uber long ago used up any goodwill it had as a company. Why should we trust Uber now?

It takes a series of incidents for a company to get a reputation like this. But in a world drenched in social media, people rapidly spread news articles, photos, and videos about incidents of poor treatment of consumers. Companies that keep screwing up—and specifically companies that have a reputation for putting their own needs before those of customers—have dug themselves a customer perception hole that's difficult to get out of.

United Airlines baggage handlers broke Dave Carroll's guitar in 2008 and refused to compensate him. The result was his song and video "United Breaks Guitars," which went viral, reaching 18 million views and laying the groundwork for United's reputation as an airline with no soul. Since then, United has: dealt with accusations of bribing officials to get more gates at Newark Airport, an incident for which the CEO resigned; suffered a failing reservation system that cancelled thousands of flights; concealed what was happening when its new CEO was having a heart attack; banned teenagers from boarding a flight because they were wearing leggings; saw its employees revolt as it tried to replace its employee bonus system with a lottery; and, famously, called airport police to drag a passenger off a plane to make room for some United employees, knocking the poor sucker unconscious in the process. A few months later, one of its flight attendants insisted a bag containing a puppy be placed in an overhead bin, where the poor animal suffocated.

Why would you trust United Airlines now?

Why would you trust Wells Fargo, a bank whose policies encouraged thousands of employees to open multiple spurious accounts in customers' names without those customers' knowledge or permission?

As security and privacy expert Fatemeh Khatibloo, principal analyst for Forrester Research, has said, "Trust is earned in drops, but lost by the bucketful."[2] As a consumer-first marketer, you are going to need that trust. You will be dealing with people's data. You will be creating offers based on that data. Do that right, and you can create a set of lasting relationships that pay off in the long term. But destroy that trust, and you lose the opportunity to build that relationship (see sidebar).

Privacy is not a problem; it's a potential competitive differentiator

The internet economy is full of paradoxes: we want free content, but we don't want to see ads; we get upset when a company captures and shares information about us, but we click "I agree" on a company's terms of service without reading it, even just to gain access to a game or quiz; and we don't like the idea of our behavior being tracked by companies, but we want messages from them to be relevant.

Consumers' perspectives on privacy are complicated. In our research, consumers sent mixed messages. Among Fully Entitled con-

sumers, 68% express concern with companies tracking their location when they are not interacting with them. At the same time, as we mentioned before, 71% tell us they would be happy if an airline popped up their boarding passes on their mobile devices as soon as they arrived at the airport, and 57% would be happy if a store they were passing by sent them an alert about a sale. Just how do they imagine these location-based features are going to work? While consumers want personalized features in their interactions with marketers, their fears are equally prominent (see table 9).

It's time to stop seeing privacy as a negative and start seeing it as a potential competitive differentiator. It then becomes the bedrock of respect, trust, and empathy, the main topics of this chapter.

Already, we see companies beginning to distinguish themselves on their treatment of customers' data. Apple and Amazon have taken advantage of Facebook's bad publicity in the Cambridge Analytica incident to promote the fact that they do not sell customer data. But we don't believe privacy needs to be weaponized to harm competitors. Every company can take positive steps to build trust and turn privacy from a feared subject to a potential competitive differentiator. Jerry Jones, chief ethics and legal officer and executive vice president of Acxiom, a major data compiler, encourages a shift in the conversation from data privacy to ethical data use. That approach requires examining privacy through an ethical and not just a legal framework.

In the rest of this chapter, we cite the importance of transparency in using consumers' data, of restraint in data collection, and of giving consumers control over how their data is used. The challenge is that when it comes to privacy and ethical data use, you must work collaboratively with other departments: your legal and regulatory compliance group and your IT department.

Table 9: Consumer are worried about how you treat their data

HOW CONCERNED ARE YOU ABOUT THE FOLLOWING COMPANY PRACTICES AND THE WAY COMPANIES TREAT YOUR INFORMATION (TOP TWO BOXES)?	OVERALL	FULLY ENTITLED
Getting 'hacked' or experiencing a data breach that exposes your data	72%	80%
Sharing your data with other companies	63%	69%
Tracking your location even when you're not interacting with them	61%	68%
Tracking your behavior on other companies' websites	56%	61%
Tracking your behavior on their website and in their apps	49%	55%
Sending you messages based on your current location or needs	49%	46%

Source: Entitled Consumer Survey.
Base: 2,000 US consumers and 1,000 consumers in each of five European countries.

- **Collaborate with compliance staff on strategies that are not just legal but beneficial.** *Privacy laws differ by country and region but are generally designed to protect consumers—lawmakers who are generally ignorant of consumer-first marketing principles have created rules that you must live within. Picking fights with your regulatory, legal, and compliance staff is a bad move—you're most likely to lose, and to the extent that you can get around them, you're putting your company at risk. Instead, start from first principles—marketing* that's in the best interests of consumers, transparent data use, consumers in control of the marketing flow—and work toward policies that are both legal and beneficial. In general, you'll find that consumer-first marketing is more compatible with data privacy regulations than traditional, repetitive, and unrestrained marketing is.

- **Maintain data security to preserve trust.** The experts at the Ponemon Institute assess the average cost to companies of a data breach is $3.6 million.[3] The damage to a company's brand may be incalculable. While data security is the responsibility of your IT team, your customer doesn't distinguish between departments—their breaches will destroy your carefully built brand. Marketing and customer service groups will want access to real-time customer data at each point of interaction—and the further data gets from being centrally stored and managed, the harder it is to secure it. So recognize that security will drive up the costs and complexity of being a consumer-first marketer, and collaborate with your IT group on solutions that are both flexible enough to fuel personalized marketing and sufficiently secure to keep data safe from black-hat hackers.

Companies that approach customer data from an ethical as well as a legal framework are in a much better position to adapt to new rules, such as Europe's GDPR. To assess your approach, consider a framework similar to the Future of Privacy Forum's open data benefit/risk assessment, which enables you to consider the benefits, reasonable expectations, and risks of accessing, keeping, and using various types of data.[4]

THE CONSEQUENCES OF MARKETING THAT LACKS RESPECT AND EMPATHY

Violations of trust, such as inappropriate sharing of data, opening accounts without permission, or knocking passengers senseless, can destroy your brand. But we'll give you the benefit of the doubt here. Let's assume that your company is already doing everything it can to prevent behavior that is this egregiously insensitive.

Even if your policies and culture prevent your staff from committing customer abuse, your marketing practices may still be communicating an insufficient degree of respect and empathy for the customers that your revenue depends on.

When it comes to marketing, the easiest thing to do is to keep doing what you have already been doing. If emails work, send more emails. If retargeting to consumers who visit your site generates business, keep showing them more ads. Send text messages. Create pointless apps. Just keep treating your customers as targets.

How would you like to be known as a "target"?

The challenge for marketers, as we described in chapter 2, is that these practices, while they demonstrate a lack of respect, actually seem to work. The more often you hit your "targets," the more your business will grow—in the short term. But overmarketing is like an addiction. Like any addict, you'll find that you must put in more and more effort, and create more and more volume, to attain the smallest additional increments of benefit.

What you haven't calculated is the long-term cost of what you are doing. So let's game that out.

First, you have tarnished your brand. Every message you send contributes to the perceptions people have about your brand. The more irrelevant impressions you make, the more they perceive your brand as one that relentlessly and cluelessly repeats itself.

Overmarketing is an **ADDICTION**—over time, you'll need to put in much more effort to get the smallest incremental benefit.

This isn't just in digital channels; it also includes companies that keep sending us useless and unwanted catalogs and repetitious direct mail pieces, or marketers who call your phone, inevitably at the least convenient moment. Behave like this, and you confirm your reputation as a loudmouthed boor. That brand perception is a lead weight you must carry around. Your brand attribute is now "pest," not "friend," and that's something you'll need to overcome.

Second, you'll be degrading your customer base. For every person who responds to one of your endlessly repeated messages, there is likely another person who became less interested in your brand and then got fed up. The fed-up person might have been looking for a relationship, but you blew that. Do that enough times, and your customer base evolves. There will be fewer people looking for the right quality products for them and more people waiting around for deals and discounts to show up. You will be appealing to the stingiest customers. You'll be like Bed Bath & Beyond, a US home-goods retailer that sends so many coupons to its customers so frequently that everyone knows they can get a discount, and no one has any urgency to go to the store any more without a coupon.[5] If you are the low-cost supplier in your market, appealing to the stingiest customers might work for you. But for the rest of the competitors in any given market, it's probably not their best positioning.

Third, you are putting your company at risk. You have expended your goodwill. At some point, something may go wrong. As we described at the top of this chapter, you may end up in a marketing scandal, like Wells Fargo; get caught creepily tracking your customers, like Uber; expose people's data to hackers, like Yahoo;

or just accidentally kill a puppy. Companies like Apple, who have stockpiled customer goodwill for decades, can withstand the occasional hiccup with antennas that don't work if you put your thumb in the wrong place or involuntary slowdowns to preserve a phone's battery life. But if you're one of those companies that has expended all its goodwill with relentless marketing messages, you have used up all your forgiveness. Your customers will be ready to believe the worst about you because you have shown them nothing else. You won't have the resources to take a hit and move on.

Overmarketing puts your company **AT RISK** because it expends all of your goodwill.

Respect and empathy are the key to retaining brand potency. They're the antidote to the tendency to overmarket and overmessage. But respect for the customer only happens when empathy is baked into the culture of your company.

If you're wondering whether your company has empathy, simply ask the question, "If I were the customer, would I find the experience delivered by my company's marketing to be valuable and useful?" If customers wouldn't react this way, you've failed the empathy test.

Some companies take the value of empathy to extremes. When Hurricane Katrina hit the Gulf Coast, bankers from Hancock Whitney set themselves up within hours on card tables outside badly damaged branches where the power was out. They gave out hundreds of dollars to customers in exchange for IOUs that were later reconciled with accounts once the power came back on. And when Baton Rouge flooded in 2016, Hancock Whitney was again one of the first banks to reopen, making disaster supplies available to customers and cashing insurance checks. It's rare that people would say a bank is empathetic, but Hancock Whitney clearly communicates those values with actions like these.

Respect for the customer only happens when empathy is baked into the **CULTURE** of your company.

But, for marketers, where respect and empathy really come through is in the way you communicate with customers. Marketing strategies that treat people more as targets than valued customers communicate a lack of empathy. When you make too many irrelevant marketing contacts, or when every message is an offer or a call to action rather than focused on the customer's need, you send the clear message, "We don't care about you."

"[After a fraud complaint] they gave me my money back straightaway. And I was like, 'Okay. The bank's got my back.' Which is one of those industries you really want to have your back. You don't want them messing around with you."

STUART, sales manager, UK

So, along with reciprocal value and relevance, respect is how to protect and preserve the consumer relationships you've built. You can embody respect in your marketing in three ways:

- **Transparency.** Be clear about what information you collect and how you use it—and how it benefits the consumer.
- **Restraint.** Don't send every message. Send only the ones most likely to benefit both the consumer and your company.
- **Control.** Allow customers to manage the cadence and channel of marketing messages.

TRANSPARENCY IS A NECESSARY PRECONDITION FOR TRUST

Marketing strategies that treat people as **TARGETS** communicate a lack of empathy.

Even as we are writing this, Facebook CEO Mark Zuckerberg is answering questions in front of the United States Congress, and the British government has written to request that Zuckerberg volunteer to appear in front of its Digital, Culture, Media, and Sport Committee or risk being subpoenaed the next time he enters the UK. Politicians in multiple countries are upset. It's painful to watch and will doubtless hurt the company by requiring it to shift many strategies, deal with potential regulation, and repair public trust. Due to both the damage to the company's brand and the cost of dealing with the fallout, Facebook's market value plummeted by $86 billion in the aftermath of the privacy scandal.

How did Facebook get itself into this position? With a lack of transparency. One of the first things Zuckerberg did, as a college student, was to create a script that pulled women's pictures off of websites for dormitories at Harvard and displayed them in an application where other students could rate how attractive they were. He didn't ask the women's permission. And sure enough, when they found out what had happened, they were upset (and Zuckerberg faced disciplinary action).

As Zeynep Tufekci described in an article in *Wired*, Facebook went on to surprise its users continually over the next fourteen years.[6] First it aggregated their activity into a newsfeed for any other members to see, with no privacy controls. It posted notes about their purchases without permission. It violated people's expectations about privacy so often that in 2011, the company was forced to sign a consent decree with the US Federal Trade Commission promising to do better. And then, in the incident that got Zuckerberg testifying in front of the US Congress, it revealed that users who had taken a personality quiz—and their online friends—had had their information collected and then exposed to Cambridge Analytica, a company that then apparently used the data to help elect Donald Trump. When Facebook enabled a feature allowing people to download and see the information that Facebook had on them, many were surprised to see logs of their phone calls and text messages included in the data dump.

Now remember, Facebook had never had a data breach—no hackers had ever gotten into its data stores. And it has not sold people's data and is unlikely ever to do so. People who took the personality quiz had to click a button to agree that it could get access to their information and their friends' information. The phone and text logs were another feature that people opted into. This is one reason that Facebook took a while to react to the outrage—because all the information people had given up, they'd actually clicked on a button to *agree* to give up.

The problem here is less about the information that was collected or even how that information was used. It's that people were *surprised* about how their information was used. People click quickly through permissions, not realizing what permissions they are giving out. So when word came out about how this information was used, people felt violated. They felt taken advantage of. Their trust was ruptured.

There is an antidote to this problem, and it is transparency. Transparency, at least so far as data collection is happening, means that no one should be surprised about the reasons that a company is collecting data or the actions that it takes with the data. A company that manifests empathy is going to be transparent about its data collection and use, because that's a sign of respect for the customer.

Here's an example. I (Josh) recently received an email offer from Amazon. Here's how it read:

> Subject: Create a free Amazon Business Account
>
> Free account includes business pricing, quantity discounts, business analytics, and more
>
> Josh, you're receiving this because you've recently placed an order on Amazon with your business-issued credit card. Create a free Amazon Business account and access exclusive business features.
>
> - Business-Only Pricing
> - Multi-User Accounts
> - Business Analytics
>
> For questions contact Business Customer Service

No one should be SURPRISED about the reasons that a company is collecting data or the actions that it takes with the data.

Amazon tends not to get into trouble for privacy violations, and the reason is transparency. There is absolutely no mystery about why I received this email—it explicitly states that I'm getting it because I used a business credit card on Amazon. No one gets this email and says, "How did you know that?"

As Brooks Dobbs, the former chief privacy officer of the agency Wunderman, told us, clarifying the value you offer in exchange for data is a winning strategy. For example, at the online site for *Wired*, you have a choice. You can see their ads. Alternatively, you can pay for the content with a subscription. If you use an ad blocker, you get a simple message about these choices. They're not coy about it; it's completely transparent.[7]

And as you create your own personalized and relevant offers for consumers, the same principle should apply. When Redfin sends an email to recent home buyers after the first time it snows on their house, no one says, "How did you know where I live? How did you know that it was snowing?"

Other marketing practices can freak people out. Fatemeh Khatibloo analyzed what consumers find creepy in her January 29, 2016, Forrester Report, "Brief: Be Cool, Not Creepy: The Causes Of Creepy Experiences And How Brands Can Avoid Them."[8] The report identifies three kinds of creepy-making corporate behaviors: perceived misuse of data (like getting drug ads after searching on a medical condition), data hygiene errors (for example, reminding someone to send Mother's Day flowers when her mother died three years ago), and invasive or aggressive tactics (like getting ads on your phone related to a search your husband made on his work computer). All three suffer from the same "how did you know that" (or "how did you not know that") problem. And that comes from a lack of transparency.

We heard complaints just like this in our focus groups. For example, Will, a Millennial, started seeing ads for popcorn machines after discussing popcorn while his phone was on the table—and he was convinced that the conversation was "heard" by marketers via his phone.

"I was searching for information on sexual health for my job. Later, I saw an ad for a discount on 100 condoms. Not cool."

BEN, nonprofit worker, US

The penalty for being creepy and lacking transparency is hard to measure, but it's real. As Brooks Dobbs asks, "How do you measure the number of people who are freaked out?" The problem is, once they are freaked out, they defect from your brand and your marketing programs. You may not know why, but your marketing programs will start driving customers away.

In contrast to this, transparency means explaining how you use information in plain language. For example, the *Guardian* newspaper in the UK is known for its extensive coverage of privacy issues. So it's no surprise that it also has one of the clearest and most transparent privacy pages on the web, including a two-minute animated video that explains in simple English the four reasons why it collects data, the information that it captures, how it uses that data, and how consumers can opt out of having that data captured. All of this builds trust, which is more critical than ever for a media company in an era of "fake news!" accusations.

Consumers are more concerned than ever of the implications of data collection, even if they don't fully understand what is happening with that data. As consumers, we know that marketers capture information about us. We're not so surprised when we get an email after we abandon a shopping cart (to some people, that's a shopping tactic) or when we see an ad for a product that we had been browsing suddenly start to "follow" us across the internet.

But as Microsoft found in research with 16,500 consumers across 13 global markets, while 56% of consumers think that brands collect personal information from them without consent, 83% expect companies to ask their permission when collecting data.[9] And while 41% of consumers in this study consciously share personal information with brands, they expect something in return: cash rewards, discounts, or appropriate new products and services. As the study concludes, "Consumers are more likely to see value in sharing data when there are obvious mutual benefits. Inconsistency in data policies and visibility of data usage can make the exchange seem one-sided. In the absence of transparency of information or clear value, the company appears to receive more benefit from collecting the data than what the consumer receives by sharing it."

> *"Don't ask too many questions. Don't make this like I'm going to outer space."*
>
> **KEISHA,** customer service rep, US

The lesson here is clear. If you collect only the data that you need—as we described in the previous chapter—and use it respectfully in ways that consumers will find transparent and valuable, you'll be perceived as helpful. If your data practices are more along the lines of "collect everything that you can, and use it to turn the consumer into a target," you'll be more of a loudmouthed boor. Choose the right path here, because your brand perception depends on it. As an added benefit, this strategy will make it easier for you to comply with new regulations like the European General Data Protections Regulation (GDPR).

As we write this, GDPR is generating widespread panic among marketers. The provisions of the new regulation require that companies must make it clear any time they are collecting data in a way that would not be obvious and explain why. GDPR also specifies that any consumer has the right to ask a company to delete the consumer's record completely—a step that immediately reduces the lifetime value of that customer to zero.

GDPR shines a spotlight on transparency, since it requires greater disclosure of what data you are collecting about a consumer and why. It places greater value on restraint, because over-messaging could cause a customer to request that she be completely deleted from your databases. And it naturally leads to preference centers where customers control their own information and manage the types and channels of marketing messages they prefer.

RESTRAINT REQUIRES DISCIPLINE BUT PAYS OFF IN THE LONG RUN

Send fewer marketing messages.

It's a very hard idea to embrace. But if you consider the plight of your consumer, it's one you have to consider. Surveys from researchers like MarketingSherpa consistently show that "too many emails" is the number one reason people unsubscribe from email lists.[10] Sure enough, when email service provider SendGrid looked at data from 50 billion marketing emails from over 100,000 senders, it found a trend: industries that increased their sending frequencies also saw a reduction in open rates and click-throughs on those emails.[11]

> *"So I will get loads of unsolicited emails from various companies. And I'll delete them. And then eventually I'll go, 'Oh my God, just unsubscribe.'"*
>
> **KAREN,** admin, UK

None of us enjoy being bombarded by irrelevant messages. Even so, we just have to turn on the TV, look in our mailbox, or switch on our smartphone to find thousands of examples a day of badly targeted communication. And the more time you spend with marketing departments, the clearer you can see the reason why. Firms typically organize around business units or product lines, and, as a result, they frequently lack a complete understanding of the value of individual customers to the company overall. Or worse: they know who those valuable customers are, but they have no idea who else within the company is communicating with them, how often, and what they are saying. (At the Swedish financial services company Folksam, as we'll describe in the following chapter, the only people who knew all the messages different departments were sending were the consumers themselves. And it was a similar lack of discipline that led to the 16 million messages sent every year to the auto club customers we described in chapter 2.)

The result of this uncoordinated communication is that the company's best customers often have the worst customer experience as they are bombarded by every business unit and channel manager with frequent, and sometimes even conflicting, messages. Entitled consumers won't stand for this.

Your **BEST** customers often have the **WORST** customer experience as they are bombarded by every business unit and channel manager with frequent, conflicting messages.

The solution is restraint. But to implement it, you need to devise and employ a consumer contact strategy or cadence management plan to coordinate who communicates with consumers and when, how, and why you communicate with them. These plans, which need to extend across business units and product lines, optimize communication to deliver the best corporate outcomes in alignment with customer preferences and value. These internal groups have to sit down together and agree on how they optimize their communications across business units and communications channels, with rules like turning off marketing when a customer is in the middle of a customer service issue (as we described in Sophia's story).

Even if firms have a primary goal to increase consumer lifetime value (LTV), they will need to map out the second-tier goals—such as customer satisfaction, loyalty and churn reduction, or the frequency or amount of spend—to optimize across teams and drive a customer's LTV.

For example, Royal Bank of Canada began by setting basic rules around frequency of communications per consumer—to send no more than one company-initiated engagement per week, for example.[12] That sounds basic in principle, but it forced the internal discussion to determine which one engagement should go out in any given week. Quickly teams found themselves working across disciplines and departments to figure out which engagements were most valuable not only to the customer but to the overall business. That internal discussion, while painful, was incredibly valuable to ultimately delivering the best possible experience to the consumer on her own terms.

And less communication does not necessarily lead to a reduction in business.

At HubSpot, the marketing team cut email volume in North America by 50% in a bid to, as CMO Jon Dick described it in a blog post, "break our addiction to email." They went down from sending two weekly emails to only one, improving the email's relevance with better segmentation, testing, and more interactive content. Engagement with the emails increased by 28%.[13]

As we described in the previous chapter, Kinepolis emails an average of 7% of its database in any given mailing. And when the Polish drugstore chain that Jan Biłyk described signs up a new customer, that customer gets no more than three messages a week. If they don't open ten consecutive emails, the drugstore stops sending emails for a month and then uses a different set of content in an email a month later to try to see if the customer might reengage.

At the language application Duolingo, once a customer fails to respond to a certain number of reminder messages, even if she actively requested the messages, the company sends a push notification to indicate that it is going to stop sending reminder notifications unless the consumer indicates that she wants to receive them. The company recognizes that the customer is not responding and that the messages might start to cause annoyance.

The financial services company Discover Financial has reevaluated how it connects with customers when they call in. It has put caps on the number of times it can contact any given customer in a year.

Kathy Hecht, CMO of Silver Star Brands, a company with multiple catalog brands, is applying the same lesson in the world of direct mail. For years, the company had seen how every time it sent a new catalog, sales increased. But the rounds of catalogs had gotten out of hand—some customers were getting successive catalogs just a few weeks apart. So, after careful testing, Hecht reduced the catalog frequency by two catalogs per year. The difference in sales has been negligible. But the difference in profit is huge, since the company is now saving over a million dollars in printing and postage. She has the marketing group focused on new goals of effectiveness and efficiency, not just volume—goals that show respect for the consumer as well.

> Less communication **DOES NOT** necessarily lead to a reduction in business.

If your company is sending uncoordinated messages to customers about many products, from many departments, or from many databases, you can't truly say you are respecting the consumer. Since you wouldn't want to be treated this way, you're not showing empathy. Pulling all that messaging together—and getting the cadence under control—is a big job. But in the long run, if you take on that job and master it, your brand will be better off, and your consumers more loyal and receptive.

CONTROL MEANS LETTING YOUR CONSUMERS DETERMINE HOW MUCH YOU MARKET TO THEM

It's a shocking idea: allow consumers to get their hands on the spigot of your marketing machine. After all, who knows what's best for consumers—the consumers themselves or the marketing experts in your company?

But when you consider that the alternative is to have the consumer unsubscribe—and cut off your channel or abandon your relationship altogether—you might see the logic in putting control in the hands of the consumer. It's the empathetic thing to do. Isn't that what you would want if you were the consumer?

Marketers have built preference centers to comply with the legal requirement that every email must enable consumers to unsubscribe. While marketers can use these same preference centers to ask consumers to sign up for communications or to clarify what they want to receive, most preference centers remain little more than a place for consumers to opt out from communications, and, as a result, marketers obscure them as much as they can from consumers.

> **A preference center creates an OPPORTUNITY to engage with consumers, learn about them, and show authentic respect.**

By contrast, progressive marketers understand that a preference center creates an opportunity to engage with consumers, to learn about them, and to show authentic respect for what's relevant to the consumer. Southwest Airlines, for example, captures key information—including a consumer's gender, date of birth, preferred travel routes, and reasons for travel—in a simple one-page form that consumers can complete in less than two minutes. It establishes a baseline of information that Southwest can augment in each future interaction with the consumer, using the progressive profiling approach we discussed in chapter 6. Other firms, such as Thomas Cook, dig deeper to understand a consumer's preferred types of vacation and offers, preferred frequency of communication, favorite destinations, and common style and method of travel. And Papa John's Pizza divides its preference center into sections of information centered around topics such as food preferences, delivery options, payment choices, and marketing preferences. It's far more extensive and therefore provides far richer data—and consumers can add to it progressively as they become more comfortable with the company.

We are big advocates of preference centers, but they are just the beginning. They establish a practice of asking the consumer her preferences, a practice that can, and should, be progressively enriched at every opportunity.

In practical terms, marketers should ask for (and infer) preferences across three dimensions: communications channel, content type, and desired frequency. Aim to understand which channels individual consumers prefer. Look at where and how they interact with you; there's a certain degree of intimacy for most consumers that differs by channel. They aren't as bothered by unsolicited direct mail but will unsubscribe from an email they don't want or mark it as spam, and they react most strongly to unwelcome text messaging because their phone is just too personal and intimate a device for most people to receive an unwanted message. But no two consumers are alike. What is okay for one might be anathema for another, hence the need to ask and verify.

Ask for (and infer) consumer preferences across THREE DIMENSIONS: communications channel, content type, and desired frequency.

Attitudes differ toward content type, too. Media companies have figured this out pretty well. They give consumers the option of getting different types of content at a really granular level. Already some newspaper and magazine companies send completely tailored newsletters based on the individual interests of each consumer. But all companies can do this. Just because a consumer hasn't told you her age, gender, or interests doesn't mean you shouldn't attempt to infer this information and her preferences based on what she opens and clicks, where she navigates, or what she searches for.

When it comes to frequency, each of us probably has a brand or two that if they emailed or texted us every day, we'd be okay with it. But that has more to do with brand affinity than our marketing communication preferences. For the majority of brands, our default preference is likely to be "less is more." Except for "daily deal"–type retailers, the desired frequency usually comes down to the value and relevance of the content. If the marketer gets the content exactly right for the recipient, the notion of frequency goes away. A major electronics retailer in the US tested sending more than a dozen emails in a week to individual consumers—all of which the company had tweaked to be extremely relevant—and saw no subsequent drop in engagement or increase in opt-outs.

Ultimately, the challenge for marketers is to think about the combination of these elements and the various permutations of content type, channel, and frequency. These permutations frequently differ based on the context of the interaction. For example, a consumer might be okay getting a credit card offer (content type) from her bank by direct mail (channel) sporadically, such as when there's something new and interesting in the market (frequency). But she might appreciate an SMS message (channel) immediately (frequency) if her balance is suddenly overdrawn (content type). Understanding the difference will make the consumer feel as though she's receiving special treatment, tailored specifically to her, and that you're delivering a service rather than trying to extract something from her. It allows the marketer to act as a friend—listening to or asking what she prefers and then watching to verify that all communications are in the consumer's best interest.

WHY RECIPROCAL VALUE, RELEVANCE, AND RESPECTFUL EMPATHY WILL POSITION YOU TO WIN

In this chapter and the two that precede it, we made the case that three elements of your marketing program will combine to give you an edge with consumer-first marketing: offering reciprocal value, maximizing the relevance of your marketing, and treating the consumer with respectful empathy.

Taken together, these strategies demand a level of discipline in marketing that's not common. They'll need advanced tools that are just becoming available from marketing technology companies, as well as a change of focus for your company.

It's a lot easier to just rely on the old marketing standbys: relentlessly advertise; hammer customers with repetitive messages; promote discounts; and sell, sell, sell.

But as more and more marketers flood every possible channel, from mobile notifications to streaming media to physical mailboxes, with more and more messages, the old strategies will lose resonance. Every time you bang the gong, the vibrations get weaker and harder to hear. Eventually, it won't pay off any more.

The only alternative will be consumer-first marketing featuring reciprocal value, relevance, and respectful empathy.

For more on what it takes to move your company toward true consumer-first marketing, read on in chapter 9.

THE CONSUMER-FIRST MARKETER'S TO-DO LIST

These are your to-dos to improve the way your company shows respectful empathy:

- ☐ Embrace data transparency: make it obvious why you collect data and how you use it.
- ☐ Resolve to send fewer marketing messages.
- ☐ Get a handle on all the groups sending messages, and develop an enterprise-wide customer contact strategy.
- ☐ Remake your preference center as a place to gather useful data, not just process opt-outs.
- ☐ Ask for and respect preferences with regard to channels, content types, and frequency.
- ☐ Collaborate with your legal/regulatory and IT groups on how to market safely and in compliance with data regulations.

PART 3

THE IMPACT OF CONSUMER-FIRST MARKETING

TOM FISH BURNE
OUR MISSION
PRETTY MUCH WHATEVER OUR COMPETITION DOES, BUT SIX MONTHS LATER
© marketoonist.com

Chapter 9

THE PATH TO CONSUMER-FIRST MARKETING

In 2001, Folksam, one of Sweden's largest insurance companies, had a problem. Customers were unhappy and were leaving. The company was so focused on selling new premiums that it lost sight of the needs of its existing customers. Its car insurance business, for example, lost 27% of its customers every year. Despite the fact that Folksam serves half of the Swedish population, the company was focused on customer acquisition and not on strengthening or growing relationships. As a result, premiums continually became more expensive for the remaining customers. As Staffan Magnehed, the executive at Folksam responsible for sales and service strategy, explained to us, Folksam didn't really understand its customers or their needs; the company's customer service was generic and didn't take a customer's specific context into consideration; and there was no retention strategy in place.

It wasn't that Folksam didn't care. It just wasn't set up as a consumer-first business. Folksam's various business units had their own strategies and communicated independently with customers. The result, according to Staffan, was "a spaghetti mess of communication." He explains, "The only one that knew about all the interactions, and all the messages, and all the offers that they had received was the customer. We had no clue. It was a catastrophe for us. They could have talked with us three times in the past week and we might have no idea, because they had used different media and had been in different places, and we might have offered them three or four different things."

Eventually, the leadership team at Folksam recognized that it had to change. The company developed a new consumer-focused business strategy aimed specifically at creating long-term, profitable customer relationships. Folksam strategically invested in improving the quality of its sales effort, predicting that it would deliver benefits in the long term. It invested in focused customer service, predicting that focus would lead to longer-lasting relationships. And it introduced a proactive customer retention strategy focused on boosting revenue by retaining the right customers.

Starting in 2008, Staffan's CRM team approached the challenge from both an inside-out and an outside-in perspective. From the inside out, they focused on understanding and acting on customer lifetime value; from the outside in, they sought to better understand customer needs and to propose appropriate solutions at the right time in order to maximize customer satisfaction. Staffan and his team made some key early decisions, starting with a recognition that the company had to act as "one Folksam" in its interaction with customers. They decided to build a customer interaction hub which, as Staffan described, would "deliver a comprehensive view of the customer's entire communication with Folksam, saving all of their interactions in one place, analyzing the chain of interactions that led to sales or cancellations, allocating customers to the right communications channel and business unit, deciding the next step during the interaction, and optimizing the interaction in terms of both cost and customer development." In other words, Folksam turned its world upside-down. It placed the customer, and her specific needs, at the center of everything the company did. It built a sophisticated customer interaction management system. And it enabled and empowered employees to help identify and solve customers' needs.

This change of focus benefited both the company and the customer. "To have a relationship with a customer and have them continue to pay us for six or seven years requires a different focus," he points out. "It requires us to want to keep the relationship and to do better things for customers. But we also know that getting a new customer costs more than four times the cost of retaining our customers, so retaining these customers benefits us too." Folksam now boasts an impressive 89% rate of customer satisfaction after a client interacts with the company. Satisfaction with customer service interactions has risen from 82% to 92% or more, depending on the channel. And the car insurance business unit's customer churn rate has dropped to 18%, now leading the business overall.

Despite how far Folksam has come, Staffan knows how far the company still has to go. "Every time we reach a milestone, we realize that the ultimate goal is even further away," he explains. "The pace of change in life is increasing, consumers are increasingly impatient, but they are also more professional and more knowledgeable. They are more connected. They want personalized and relevant service. And they even want greater control over what we

You must understand every dimension of the **TRANSITION** to being a consumer-first business and evaluate your place in that transition.

sell—not just how we sell it." Staffan recognizes the need to invest further to evolve Folksam's data management and interaction management capabilities. He wants to expand Folksam's capabilities in identity resolution, to improve digital asset and content management, to embrace contextual intelligence, and to stay ahead of privacy and legislative changes, because being a consumer-first business requires constant adaptation and improvement.

THE CONSUMER-FIRST MATURITY FRAMEWORK

The level of consumer-first marketing that Staffan and the team at Folksam achieved is not an accident. It is not a byproduct of some other activity. Folksam has been successful because it took a systematic approach to the goal of creating long-term, profitable customer relationships. Teams at Folksam came together and actively plotted a course to achieve this vision.

How can you do the same? You must understand every dimension of the transition to being a consumer-first business and evaluate your place in that transition. That's what this chapter is about. While not every company will follow the same path, and not every company will strive for the same destination, you need to know the milestones along that path.

That's why we created a consumer-first marketing maturity framework. Using it, you can:

- **Identify your organization's current state of maturity.** You can't make progress on attaining consumer-first marketing without understanding your starting point. Evaluating your company with this maturity framework can uncover blind spots inside the organization. Periodic evaluations will provide a benchmark to assess improvements over time as your organization evolves.

- **Align on your destination and goals.** For some organizations, achieving success in all these criteria may not be possible or even desirable. The maturity model provides the framework to discuss your ideal level of consumer-first maturity and to connect it with strategic plans for growth.

- **Build a roadmap to achieve those goals.** Once you know where you're starting from and where you're trying to go, you can more easily begin to identify what's needed to get there. Don't just think in terms of data and technology; also consider organizational structures, employee incentives, training needs, and internal processes.

- **Prioritize investments.** While a roadmap provides a blueprint for what you want to build, you'll need to work with your finance team to analyze costs and benefits. You might find dependencies that demand prioritizing some areas before others. We also recommend identifying projects that will generate immediate benefit to the business and to the consumer. These early wins will generate political goodwill to sustain you as you pursue initiatives with longer-term benefits.

- **Track results for continuous improvement.** You should reevaluate your progress at regular intervals. Some of our clients complete their company's assessment every six months. Regular assessments create the opportunity to

Early consumer-first marketing wins generate political **GOODWILL** to sustain you as you pursue initiatives with longer-term benefits.

evaluate progress, realign goals, and celebrate successes along the way. They'll also reveal where you can add new questions to the maturity framework as the market, consumers, and the business evolve.

Our goal in this chapter is to give you the tools to build a maturity framework that makes sense for your business. How you assemble them is up to you.

THE FIVE DIMENSIONS OF THE CONSUMER-FIRST MARKETING JOURNEY

As you evaluate your position on the path to consumer-first marketing, you must assess your progress on five dimensions:

- **Strategy.** How aligned is your corporate strategy with the principles of consumer-first marketing?
- **Customer knowledge.** Are your systems designed so you can understand your consumers?
- **Customer experience.** Are your efforts delivering the optimal experience to consumers?
- **Customer engagement.** Are your communications with consumers personalized and effective?
- **Measurement.** How will you measure your progress?

Let's take a closer look at what's included in each of these dimensions.

Strategy sets the direction

As we've described throughout this book, building relationships with entitled consumers isn't about leveraging a new channel, sending a different message, or adopting a new technology stack. Consumer-first marketing is about a new approach. Without a solid strategy, your efforts will not cohere. The following are the elements of consumer-first marketing strategy:

Building relationships with entitled consumers ISN'T about leveraging a new channel, sending a different message, or adopting a new technology stack.

- **Consumer-first planning.** Consumer-first marketing happens only with deliberate and focused planning. Folksam, for example, stepped back from its previous approach and plotted a new course for the business. This was way more than a mission statement: the company determined where it wanted to go and put processes, procedures, and investments in place to get there. Similarly, as we described in chapter 6, T-Mobile completely revamped its approach to one focused on eliminating consumer pain points. At companies like Folksam, T-Mobile, Discover Financial, and USAA, company strategy now focuses on recognizing the consumer and her needs. Assess your planning with these questions: *Is understanding and meeting consumer needs a priority at the board and executive levels? Is it a focus of executive team meetings along with finance and sales? Is there a defined strategy that places the consumer, and delivering value to her, as a primary focus for the business?*

- **Organizational readiness.** Regardless of whether you are organized around products, lines of business, department functions, or customer segments, organizational silos are inevitable. But the consumer doesn't care about your internal plumbing. Your strategy must acknowledge the silos and put processes and incentives in place to ensure the consumer doesn't suffer because of the organizational structure. As we described in the previous chapter, the large Canadian bank RBC modeled the value of each communication to its customers across all lines of business and used that model to manage communications limits across the whole company. Assess your organizational readiness with these questions: *Do business units and channel teams compete for the attention of consumers? Does the company measure, predict, and evaluate the impact of individual interactions with consumers? Are there incentives to encourage business units and channel managers to work together in the interest of the consumer?*

- **Budget allocation.** Understanding and meeting the consumer's needs requires a new budgeting approach. Companies need to research the consumer, listen to her voice, reconsider how they capture and analyze consumer data, make consumer insights available at the point of interaction, and leverage those insights in consumer interactions. As we described in chapter 3, Disney Parks & Resorts invested more than a billion dollars in a top-to-bottom overhaul of how the company understands, interacts, and delivers value to its guests. While companies don't have to invest a billion dollars as Disney did, the consumer-first transformation demands a significant budget. Assess your budget allocation with these questions: *Do we invest in capturing the voice of the customer and understanding her needs in a given moment? Do we calculate and communicate the value we deliver to customers? Is there an assigned budget to fund the customer-centric transformation?*

- **External factors.** Businesses use tools like SWOT and PEST analyses or Michael Porter's Five Forces to understand changes in their competitive market.[1] But we don't often see firms consider external factors through a consumer-first lens. T-Mobile, for example, used the inflexibility of competitors' mobile contracts in the United States to introduce consumer-centric initiatives and gain market share. Assess external factors with these questions: *Does our organization look for unmet customer needs in the market? Do we consider the impact of technological advancements or changes in consumer behaviors on customer expectations? Do we measure the consumer-first behavior of our competitors?*

- **Adaptive culture.** Consumer relationships change continuously. This constant flux requires companies not just to understand the consumer's situation but to be able to react to it in real time. Assess your adaptive culture with these questions: *Do we have a test-and-learn culture? Do we seek to understand customer needs and respond in real time? Does our organization leverage machine learning and artificial intelligence, optimization, and testing to continuously understand and adapt to what the consumer wants and needs?*

Unless you are a senior executive at your company, it's unlikely that you have direct influence over the annual strategic planning process, but there is plenty you can do at a departmental and individual contributor level. Start to map out the costs and benefits of your practices. Ally with someone in finance to dig into the numbers. Map the implications of consumer-first activities on your company's key financial metrics. Can you show, for example, how a change in customer satisfaction drives retention, or how sending fewer outbound communications actually improves revenue for your business line? Use this evidence to justify your efforts and attain permission to delve deeper.

Customer knowledge is the lifeblood of consumer-first marketing

Data is the fuel that drives consumer-first marketing. It is data and the insights you can derive from it that enable you to better understand the consumer and to put the exact information she's looking for in front of her, at the exact moment she is looking for it. The following are the elements of customer knowledge as a dimension of consumer-first marketing:

- **Data capture.** As we described in chapter 4, four types of data power consumer-first marketing: descriptive data, such as demographics and preferences; social connections in real life and on social media; relationship history relating to purchases, returns, customer service, and interactions in all channels; and situational data, such as local weather, traffic, or sports results. Recall how the Belgian retailer JBC captures data ranging from the types of articles a consumer buys and her language preferences to customers' birthdays and their local weather. Assess your data capture with these questions: *Do we capture all forms and types of data that would be useful to serve the customer with maximum relevance? Do we capture data that we don't need, that we should stop capturing?*

- **Data integration.** It's one thing to capture various types of data, but it's another to integrate them and make insights usable for marketing purposes. For example, as we described in chapter 4, the medical publisher Wyanoke integrated data across all its 40 publications and events to fully understand customer engagement for its 2 million contacts. Marketers don't need a fully integrated set of customer data to deliver on consumer-first marketing, but they do need a mechanism to tap in to other systems to integrate just the right data to make a decision. Assess your data integration with these questions: *Have we* *mapped our data assets to understand which data we should integrate? Do we understand the dynamic nature of data—which data needs to be available in real time versus data that remains valid for longer periods of time? Do we structure and normalize our data so that it can be accessed by a central system and leveraged broadly?*

- **Customer intelligence.** Data on its own has limited value. By applying analytics to it, though, marketers can ask and answer a broad range of questions. For example, financial services firms like Discover Financial examine patterns not only to predict fraud but also to predict the next best action, such as what message to present to the consumer based on her needs in the moment. Descriptive analytics can determine how valuable different customers might be or what products are most often bought together. Predictive analytics takes insight to the next level by making predictions, such as which content will deliver the most value to a given customer, where someone is most likely to see an important message, or which customers are most likely to respond to a given offer. Assess your customer intelligence with these questions: *Do we use descriptive analytics to understand patterns in our customer data? Do we use predictive analytics to forecast the best actions for the company to take? Do we continuously evolve our models to accommodate insights and additional data points as they become available?*

- **Access to intelligence.** The best customer intelligence sitting in a report or dashboard, interesting as it may be, is largely wasted if it's not accessible at the point of interaction. For example, at one American financial services firm, a bank teller sees a red, yellow, or green indicator for a consumer based on her lifetime value and uses the information to inform their conversation. The teller doesn't need to read why the consumer got that color to know whether to attempt to upsell the consumer or focus more on areas of satisfaction or dissatisfaction. Assess your company's access to intelligence with these questions: *Do we make intelligence available where it is needed? Is the intelligence provided in a consumable form for each group that accesses it? Is it up to date and relevant at the point of interaction so that it can guide decisions most accurately?*

- **Flexibility.** Advanced companies marry known data with real-time observations and empower their employees to act on the data and insights to serve their customers—like the first-class bartenders on Emirates Airlines who use knowledge from earlier flights to deliver more empathetic service. Assess your company's flexibility with using data with these questions: *Do we have the means to quickly and easily integrate data to guide relationship marketing decisions? Do our systems and models update in real time when employees add new data and intelligence to them? Do we have structures in place to allow employees to act on customer intelligence during a live interaction?*

Customer data is a tangible business asset. In fact, several years ago, I (Dave) advocated for firms accounting for it on their balance sheets, an idea that is beginning to gain traction.[2] But capturing the data isn't enough; firms must also generate intelligence from it and make it available to employees who are empowered to use it to make a difference in how they communicate with, and deliver value to, consumers.

Customer experience reflects a consumer's perception of your brand

> Capturing the data isn't enough; you must generate intelligence from it and **EMPOWER** employees to use that intelligence for the benefit of customers.

In the final analysis, what matters most is not how well you think you are doing at personalizing interactions, understanding consumer needs, delivering exceptional customer service, and meeting and exceeding your consumer's expectations. What matters is whether it leads to a better customer experience. The following are the elements of customer experience as a dimension of consumer-first marketing:

- **Empathy.** When Hancock Whitney Bank set up card tables in front of branches that were damaged in hurricanes and gave out money in exchange for IOUs, as we described in chapter 8, the primary motive was not profit. Hancock Whitney's bankers did this because they cared about what their customers were going through. They showed empathy for their customers in a way that was both simple and profound. You don't have to wait for a hurricane to put yourself in the consumer's shoes. For example, as we described in chapter 4, Coolblue recognized that consumers needed help with their recent purchases and sent timely videos explaining products, which both helped consumers and reduced returns. Assess your company's empathy with these questions: *Do we seek to understand our customers' emotional states when interacting with them? How well do we understand our customers' needs in any given moment? How flexible are our processes to enable employees to resolve customer needs outside our standard business operating procedures?*

- **Customer journeys.** As we discussed in chapter 5, consumers don't follow a linear path down the funnel from discovery through purchase to loyalty. They choose when, where, and how they will interact with you. You must respect their decisions and meet them in the moment. You must think through the journeys or paths that a consumer might take and seek to remove any friction from the process. When this is most effective, you can streamline their path, like American Airlines when it estimates the time it will take to get to the airport at the moment when you're popping up your boarding pass. Assess your approach to customer journeys with these questions: *Are our journeys dynamic and adaptive to allow for the broadest possible number of potential interactions with a customer? Are they flexible enough to start and end on a consumer's terms, rather than expecting her to begin and end where we think they should? Can they trigger a response based on a consumer state rather than a linear action?*

- **Customer and product lifecycle.** Consider an electronics retailer that understands where each consumer is in her lifecycle with each major purchase. For example, the electronics retailer knows that a consumer bought her TV one year ago, her phone six months ago, and her laptop three years ago. The store customizes its communications around each of these products by understanding, for example, that the consumer is unlikely to replace her phone for another year or so but might appreciate tips on how to keep it operating quickly or about what accessories she might appreciate. Assess your approach to customer lifecycles with these questions: *Do we know the average lifecycle for our products and services? Do we know which customers follow the average lifecycle and which are likely to change or upgrade sooner or later than the average?*

Think through the journeys or paths that a customer might take, and seek to remove any **FRICTION** from the process.

Do we have ways to deliver value to customers between their purchase cycles?

- **Customer preferences.** Preference management includes more than just how frequently a consumer wants to hear from you. It can extend to progressive profiles of that consumer: what she likes to receive, when she typically responds, and which types of communication seems to deliver the most value to her. For example, as we described in chapter 7, the cinema chain Kinepolis keeps a profile of consumer-declared preferences as well as a profile with observed and inferred preferences of each consumer. Assess your approach to customer preferences with these questions: *Do we give customers the chance to declare their preferences to us in an easy manner? Do we think broadly about what the customer prefers as it relates to interacting with our company and not just about frequency and channel of communication? Do we emphasize what we believe to be the customer's preference as a priority in deciding how and when to interact?*

- **Omnichannel experience.** The consumer doesn't care about your internal organization or why one department doesn't know that some other department interacted with her just the day before. As Staffan Magnehed remarked about Folksam's former approach, sometimes the customers are the only ones who know when and how often your company has interacted with them. And, more often than not, that will make you look like an inconsiderate boor. Assess your omnichannel experience with these questions: *Do we capture interactions in real time across all channels? Can we adapt in one channel to what we learn about a customer in another? Do we coordinate messages, offers, and interactions with customers based on every previous interaction, regardless of where they occurred?*

Customer engagement brings personalization to life

As we explained in chapter 5, firms that apply an adaptive customer engagement strategy can deliver exactly what is most likely to be of help or interest to the consumer at any given moment and in whatever channel the consumer is using to interact. This is where it all comes together: the customer intelligence, atomized content, and interaction capability to deliver the most relevant, valuable, and respectful message in the most welcome way to the consumer. The following are the elements of customer engagement as a dimension of consumer-first marketing:

- **Identity recognition.** Remember how I (Josh) used my credit card in the Amazon store, and it automatically recognized me and gave me the appropriate discount? Or how Google remembers what you do on your phone app and updates on your desktop? These types of interactions depend on identifying, recognizing, and remembering the customer. Only then can you can apply all the rules and run all the algorithms to determine the right content to deliver. Assess your identity recognition with these questions: *Do we use a mix of probabilistic and deterministic approaches to recognize customers? Can we quickly identify customers regardless of the channel in which they interact? Can we associate anonymous behavior with a known customer once she is identified—in a respectful manner?*

- **Context awareness.** Gartner often talks about "two-speed" marketing, a term that describes operating at a speed that focuses on the long-term need to build an overarching brand, as well as the need to respond in the moment to a consumer's specific context.[3] Being context aware allows a marketer to respond to a consumer's need in her exact situation. Assess your context awareness with these questions: *Do we seek to understand a customer's* *appropriate context information (e.g., location, time of day, or device) and use the information to understand the customer's broader situation, such as the weather, the time until she departs, or the distance from the nearest store? Do we update our message and content based on a customer's context in real time? Do we take real-time business context, such as inventory or hours of operation, into consideration when interacting with consumers?*

- **Atomized content.** In chapter 5, we discussed how Disney determines whether to send images of princesses, Star Wars characters, or pirates based on what the company knows about consumers. Disney can do this because it takes an atomized approach to content, with appropriate assets ready to deploy based on the consumer's current situation. Assess your capability around atomized content with these questions: *Do we have the right metadata to describe our content in such a way that we can assemble it as necessary? Is our content usable across channels, devices, and screen sizes? Do we have the right technology to assemble content on the fly based on all the knowledge we have about the interaction—what we know about the customer and her need in the moment?*

- **New forms of engagement.** High-end resorts allow you to check them out via virtual reality so that you can explore the property and get a feel for the experience before signing up. Sometimes it seems like every other week there's a new approach to marketing for CMOs and their teams to contend with, from mixed reality apps and devices to bots, voice-based devices, and wearables. Marketers need to figure out how to embrace these new communications vehicles without abandoning their approach to customer engagement. Assess your approach to new forms of engagement with these questions: *Do we take a methodical approach to embracing new channels,* *extending our existing approach as appropriate for the channel? Do we have a method of assessing the effectiveness of new channels as they emerge to avoid chasing every shiny object? Can we apply our consumer-first approach to new channels, ensuring we capture the right data and apply existing customer knowledge in these interactions?*

- **Engagement beyond marketing.** While this book is written for marketers, we know marketing teams must work hand in hand with other customer-facing departments. The consumer doesn't distinguish between your marketing, customer support, or finance teams, and you shouldn't expect them to. Folksam needed to invest in a renewed sales and service strategy, not just in marketing, as it evolved to become a consumer-first company. Departments must connect—that's the only way to deliver experiences like the ones we showed in Sophia's story in chapter 3, where a customer service representative was able to suppress marketing until a damaged product was replaced. Assess your capability for engagement beyond marketing with these questions: *Do we have a consistent view of the customer across all our internal departments? Can the activities in one department affect how other departments interact with a customer in real time? Are our departments incented to work together to benefit the customer?*

Measurement keeps you on course

If you can't measure it, you can't manage it. You've heard it before, and we're saying it again. Unless you measure the business impact of your consumer-first efforts, they will appear as a Pollyanna-esque crusade toward nice, feel-good things to do for customers. Good luck getting your CFO and CEO on board with that! The following are the elements of consumer-first marketing measurement:

- **Consumer-first metrics.** Too many marketers continue to focus on operational metrics that have limited impact on the business, such as open rates and clickthrough rates. The first step to measuring—and subsequently improving—consumer-first marketing is to measure relevant performance indicators such as customer satisfaction, retention rates, advocacy or loyalty rates, and customer value delivered. One financial services firm we spoke to told us that it ranks customers from one star to five stars based on their value to the company—and the firm has figured out that a five-star customer is worth as much to the business as 700 one-star customers! While some of the marketers we've interviewed measure satisfaction or Net Promoter Score, few examine advanced metrics such as value delivered. Assess your consumer-first metrics with these questions: *Are we relying on operational metrics to measure the impact of our marketing programs? Do we measure consumer-first metrics, such as satisfaction or customer value delivered? If not, do we have what we need to begin measuring these metrics?*

Unless you measure the **BUSINESS IMPACT** of your consumer-first efforts, they will appear as a Pollyanna-esque crusade toward nice, feel-good things to do for customers.

- **Customer value.** Since the late 1980s, experts have been advocating for businesses to measure and improve customer lifetime value (LTV). Some firms, such as Farmers Insurance in the United States, use LTV to guide a broad set of business decisions, ranging from the type of agents to hire—by analyzing the background of agents who acquire customers with higher LTV—to which customers to move to a self-service model to maximize profitability.[4] Assess your approach to customer value with these questions: *Do we measure LTV? If not, do we have* *what we need to begin to measure it? What do we need to do to get organizational support for measuring and managing customer LTV?*

- **Business impact.** By itself, satisfaction is not an economic metric. Regardless of how satisfied customers are, what matters most is how they behave toward your brand. While it's important to measure consumer-first metrics, it's critical to tie them to economic metrics, such as incremental loyalty or LTV. As Murli Buluswar, former chief science officer at AIG and now a senior executive advisor at Boston Consulting Group, told us, "It's not enough to just look at how feeling changes, or what drives satisfaction. Firms should measure what drives loyalty. If we can determine what causes the customer to act differently—to vote with their wallets—then we can invest to improve in these areas. When I predict what future loyalty I can expect from a certain person, and whether certain company actions would improve or damage that expected loyalty, then I can make much more informed decisions that will actually impact my top and bottom line." Assess your ability to measure business impact with these questions: *Do we connect consumer-first metrics with economic metrics to understand the business impact of our consumer-first initiatives? Do we know what corporate behaviors drive incremental loyalty and LTV? Do we invest based on the expected impact on loyalty and LTV?*

- **Organizational buy-in.** If you want the business to move toward a more consumer-first mindset, you're going to have to take on a second job as an evangelist. Look for sympathetic ears inside the organization—the CFO, for one—who can help you explain the impact of consumer-first activities. Several years ago, when Aaron Cano was VP of enterprise customer knowledge at 1-800-FLOWERS, he shared insights with business line GMs about their businesses. Some, in turn, began to report these metrics to the COO in their check-in meetings. Soon, other GMs were knocking on Aaron's door and looking for the same analyses because the COO was now inquiring about them in their own businesses. The best part? Aaron had been knocking on the doors of those same GMs just a few months earlier, trying to convince them to adopt the additional metrics. Assess your organizational buy-in with these questions: *Do we produce metrics about the business that other parts of the company can use to plan and manage consumer-first activities? Is the information easy to consume and readily accessible for all relevant parts of the business? Does the organization understand and know how to leverage the insights we share?*

- **Adaptation.** Analysis and insights matter only if you can apply them to change the business. Those changes could be as significant as changing your products and services or as simple as changing the content of your messages. Ultimately, marketers should aim to simulate what is likely to happen when they take certain actions and then measure what actually ends up happening to compare predictions with actual results. Assess your ability to adapt with these questions: *Do we have processes in place to quickly adjust to information we learn about our customers and the impact of our marketing? Do we leverage a blend of human, rules-based, and artificial intelligence to gain a broad understanding of our activities? Do we have the right technology in place to quickly adapt to what we learn to better serve the customer in the moment?*

TURNING THE FRAMEWORK INTO A MATURITY MODEL

These questions are not meant to be an exhaustive list. For example, you might add questions that are specific to your industry. Or you may need to add questions as new technology or consumer behavior affects your relationship with consumers. In our experience, questioning your organization's level of maturity in the consumer-first transformation provides value not just in the answers but in the process. When one team or colleague believes that the company is advanced in a given area while others believe it to be a laggard, the resulting conversation and ultimate alignment will leave both groups better off than they were before.

To create a true maturity model, not just a framework, you'll need to create scores for your company in each of these areas. To be precise about your assessment, you'll have to survey your people about how well you are doing. When thinking about how to precisely measure your response in each area, consider one of three approaches:

1. **Agree/disagree statements.** Create a set of statements that indicate how well your company matches up to the criteria we've listed here. Then survey your own staff about how well your company lives up to those statements. Expect to have multiple statements relating to each subject. For example, on the topic of data capture, you would ask multiple questions about the types of data that the business captures.

2. **Sophistication statements.** Alternatively, you can try to define what sophistication might look like with statements that describe how different companies might perform. Each statement would indicate an increase

in sophistication and receive a higher corresponding score as a result. In the data-capture example, it might begin with "we capture demographic data about the customer," which might receive a score of 1. The next level might include questions about various channels, and at the highest level, you might state, "We capture the broadest possible understanding about our customers, including their demographics, interests, past behavior, and their current situation, which allows us to make real-time inferences about their needs." Your respondents would then select the statement that most accurately reflects your company's current state of sophistication, and your model would register the corresponding score for that criterion.

Consumer-first transformation isn't an edifice you must build one brick at a time; it's more like a ROADMAP for all the dimensions in which you can improve.

3. **Prevalence of a capability.** Finally, you can build a maturity model based on Carnegie Mellon University's capability maturity model.[5] This approach would pose the most sophisticated statement (as we described above) and ask respondents within the organization about how prevalent that notion is inside the organization. Is it something that never occurs or doesn't exist, something that is sporadic or dispersed in pockets of the organization, or something that is frequent, consistent, or systematic within the organization?

ATTAINING CONSUMER-FIRST MATURITY IS A LONG PROCESS

If you are a true believer in the consumer-first marketing concept, you may have found this chapter a bit overwhelming. Don't think of it as an edifice you must build one brick at a time. Think of it as a roadmap for all the dimensions and elements in which you can improve.

Review what we've said about strategy, customer knowledge, customer experience, customer engagement, and measurement. Determine where your company is in good shape and where a change could make the biggest and most powerful impact. And line up colleagues who believe in the same thing to work on other parts of the framework.

Remember, consumer-first marketing is a unique source of competitive advantage. Such advantages don't come easy. But once you get them, they create a permanent, defensible competitive position. They create actual loyalty. That's why Folksam's churn rate is now so much lower—and yours could be, too.

THE CONSUMER-FIRST MARKETER'S TO-DO LIST

These are your to-dos for assessing your consumer-first transformation:

- ☐ Resolve to begin a systematic assessment of your company's progress on becoming a consumer-first marketer.
- ☐ Assess your strategy, including planning, organizational issues, budgets, competitive situation, and culture.
- ☐ Assess your customer knowledge, including what data you capture, how you integrate it, how you apply the insights from it in real time, how you expose those insights, and your level of flexibility around data.
- ☐ Assess your customer experience, including your level of empathy; your approach to customers' journeys, lifecycles, and preferences; and the experience across channels.
- ☐ Assess how you interact with consumers, including how you recognize them, address their context, deliver atomized content to them, engage with them across all departments, and address emerging modes of engagement.
- ☐ Assess what you measure, including consumer-first metrics, customer LTV, business impact, organizational buy-in, and adaptability.
- ☐ Develop organizational surveys to turn these assessments into a maturity model.
- ☐ Use these assessments to develop a shared understanding and figure out where to concentrate your efforts.

THE FUTURE OF ADVERTISING
LIGHTBULBS ARE ON SALE, ONLY $3.65
YOU'RE RUNNING LOW ON ALMOND MILK
68
BUY THIS SHIRT IN FALL COLORS
DISTRACTED? TRY RITALIN
GET AWAY FROM IT ALL WITH CHEAP FLIGHTS TO ARUBA
YOU COULD SAVE $126 ON HEATING
NEXT TIME, TRY BACON CHEDDAR RANCH
ANXIETY? TRY XANAX
LIKE THESE SNEAKERS? TRY THE RUNNING SHOES
THIS ROOM COULD SMELL LIKE WHITE TEA AND LILY
TOM FISH BURNE
© marketoonist.com

Chapter 10

THE CONSUMER-FIRST FUTURE

Drew Green runs a company that is growing at 50% per year in one of the world's toughest markets: retail. Consumer-first marketing is at the center of his success.

The global retail market is collapsing. In a short time, scores of companies around the world, including historical stalwarts like Toys "R" Us, RadioShack, Sports Authority, and Claire's have gone bankrupt; Macy's and Sears are closing stores left and right. Challenger, Gray & Christmas, a job placement firm, calculates that traditional retailers have announced over 200,000 layoffs between 2013 and 2017.[1]

Drew Green's company, Indochino, sells custom men's suits along with shirts, blazers, vests, and pants. Given the casual workplace trend that has swept through offices across the planet, men's suits would be the last place you would think to look for growth.

Drew Green isn't worried about that. He's focused on providing customers with exceptional experiences that will keep them coming back for more.

Indochino is aggressive in bricks-and-mortar retail. The company opened its first permanent store in 2015 and had 19 retail showrooms at the end of 2017. By the end of 2018, that number will almost double. Drew Green isn't worried about the retail apocalypse—it makes it cheaper for him to get deals with landlords, which makes it easier to reach customers.

The men's suit business traditionally revolves around inventory and designers. The suits come in with the designers' names on them. The salespeople glad-hand the customers and then steer them toward what's in stock. It's a merchandise-first approach.

Indochino has turned that model on its head. Indochino has no designers. It has no inventory. Freed from those constraints, it can give a man the exact suit he wants.

When you enter an Indochino showroom—whether as a walk-in in response to an ad or by appointment—you connect with a Style Guide. A Style Guide is an employee whose job is to help you get the suit *you* want, not the suit he has in stock. He shows you fabrics, colors, and patterns. He can customize your lapels, buttons, linings, and monograms. Most importantly, he measures you carefully, taking 14 different body measurements and choosing one of three silhouettes for you. Then the Style Guide enters your fabric and style choices into an app on his iPad. From there, your order goes to an overseas production facility, which creates the exact suit you asked for. The suit typically costs $399, a price for which you'd be hard pressed to get a run-of-the-mill, off-the-rack "designer" suit in a menswear store. Three weeks after you order, your custom-made suit shows up. It looks great, and it fits like it was made for you—because it was. Customers like that. Indochino's return rate hovers around a barely measurable 1%.

The showroom at Indochino is not a sales floor. The showroom is the start of a relationship. As Drew puts it, "retail is our number one marketing channel." Customers can start in a store and then confidently order more garments online.

Indochino spends money on advertising in a diverse set of print and online channels to get you into that showroom. The average cost to acquire a customer is $80. That can't go to waste. So selling one suit isn't the goal. Developing a lifelong relationship is.

Once you have bought a suit, Indochino knows you will probably buy again. As Drew told us, "We have one of the richest data sets of any retail commerce company." As a result, you won't get generic messages. You get what you're most likely to be looking for.

Indochino knows your measurements. It knows whether you like wool or blended, plaid or pinstripe, blue or gray or brown or purple. (Yes, they can carry tasteful shades of purple when there's no need to worry about inventory.) When you get an email from Indochino, it won't show you double-breasted suits if you like narrow lapels with three buttons. It won't show you flat-front pants if you like pleats. And when you visit Indochino.com, you'll see the suits, shirts, and accessories that match what you already picked out personally, what you've bought and look great in.

Indochino is smart about those emails. First off, you won't get any solicitations within the first 30 days of receiving your suit, because that's too soon—a suit is a major investment. After that, you get messages suited to you. If you open them, they continue. If you don't open them, they slow down for a while.

If you live in San Francisco and you're visiting Austin, you might see an Indochino ad. The ad will be about visiting the showroom in Austin. Drew and his marketers know that you might have some downtime in Austin that you'd like to use to get another custom-made suit, or shirt, or the tie that matches what you bought before. And if you show up in that showroom, the Style Guide will have all your information and measurements ready on his iPad, so you don't have to waste time explaining what you like, even though he's never seen you before.

The results of a customer-first attitude at Indochino are startling. The average customer buys a second garment within 90 days. The company sells half a million garments per year, all made to order. Indochino grew sales fivefold between 2014 and 2017; its annual sales growth has exceeded 50%, making it one of the five fastest-growing apparel brands in the world. Two-thirds of its customers are Millennials. (Yes, that's right, Millennials in custom-made suits.) And unlike most high-growth companies, it's profitable.

The key elements of Indochino's strategy are virtual inventory, a focus on experience over transactions, and relentless personalization, not just in its made-to-order product but also in its customized marketing approach. Indochino lives the consumer-first principles of reciprocal value, relevance, and respect. The men who walk into its showrooms, open its emails, and peruse its website appear to be responding.

PREPARE FOR THE CONSUMER-FIRST WORLD

Indochino's approach is not out of reach for your company. As we've explained in the first nine chapters of this book, consumer-first marketing principles can work in your business. As more and more companies adopt those principles, both consumers and marketers will see the world differently. So let's take a tour through a world where entitled consumers reward companies like Indochino that take the consumer-first marketing approach and punish the rest.

Marketing will focus on creativity, strategy, and technology rather than campaigns

Consumer-first marketing will remake the job of marketing.

Right now, CMOs and senior marketers focus on marketing strategy, while the marketing rank and file spends its time on campaigns—creative, timing, launches, and measurement. That's about to change.

Consumer-first marketing focuses on using all available data to deliver personalized messages in the right channel at the right moment. No human can manage that. Only an automated system can. And increasingly, automated systems built on AI will decide what marketing happens.

No more will human marketers decide what campaign to launch, pressing the send button and then anxiously observing the results. That will be the machine's job. Just as at Indochino, an algorithm will determine when to email, text, or send an app notification; what pictures, messages, and offers to show; how the website reacts to a consumer's visit; and what to display on ads.

So what will the people in marketing do?

They will set the strategy, and not just at the most senior level. Midlevel marketing managers will tweak the algorithms, analyze the results, and determine new directions for the brand and new consumer-first ideas. They'll keep the consumer-first marketing machine moving in fresh and positive directions, even as it reaches

FUTURE marketing departments will focus on strategy, creative, and technology, not on marketing campaigns.

out with thousands or millions of individual communications to individual consumers.

They will design the creative. People have taste. They have ideas. They understand brands. Their creativity will power the brand, not just by architecting a top-level brand vision (Nike's "Just Do It," McDonald's "Lovin' It"), but by creating a vast collection of media assets for the consumer-first algorithms to use. Marketing staff will design, draw, take photographs, shoot and edit video, and write copy. The demand for these skills will only increase, because the consumer-first marketing machine runs on atomized content.

And people will build the data and technology engine that delivers these marketing interactions. Data and technology professionals will be equal partners with strategy and creative, because you can't do modern consumer-first marketing without sophisticated technology.

Marketers will also become primary interfaces with product developers. This is nothing new—in packaged goods companies like Procter & Gamble, marketing and product development have always worked hand in hand. But now the product developers and marketers will pore over results of consumer-first marketing engagements, looking for clues on new consumer segments, new kinds of demand, and new ways to enhance products with mobile and digital elements.

Tomorrow's strategy, creative, and marketing technology hires will need to understand the interplay among these disciplines. Marketing schools will need to teach differently, immersing students in teams including all of these elements, rather than assigning ritualized, and increasingly obsolete, campaign-based exercises. The next generation of marketing managers will need to master machine learning, marketing automation, and data management alongside traditional lessons in the four Ps. Look for business schools in tech-heavy areas, like Silicon Valley, Boston, London, and Berlin, to shift their focus to training the next generation of technology-driven marketers.

Data trust becomes a brand attribute

Walmart is about great prices. Amazon is about convenience and comprehensive selection. Volvo is about safety. Apple is about clever design and technology.

But not all brand attributes are positive—some brands acquire attributes through their behavior rather than on purpose. Ryanair is cheap and insensitive. Comcast is about customer service frustration. Sears is frayed at the edges.

Another brand attribute will soon add itself to companies' brand image. Entitled consumers working with a brand will ask themselves, "Does this company use my data to put my needs first, or to harass me?"

Some digital brands are already leading here. Google has, for the most part, treated customers' data well and used it to benefit those customers. So has Apple. But those attributes will now spread to nondigital brands as well.

Companies like Indochino, USAA, and Kinepolis will get a boost as they do business with consumers. The trust they have earned will put them in the position to grow their loyal customer bases.

In contrast, as we described in chapter 8, companies like Yahoo, Uber, and Wells Fargo have not proven themselves to be faithful stewards of people's information. In the age of social media, word about them will spread rapidly. When consumers' decisions are based on a company's reputation, these companies will increasingly lose out to competitors.

The companies on the downside of the trust equation will pay a real penalty. They'll have to attract customers with tactics other than consumer-first marketing, because customers won't trust them with their data. There are two obvious strategies for companies like this to succeed: discounting and advertising. Both are expensive. And both cut deeply into company profits.

Shifting consumer attitudes will divide brands into consumer-first leaders and laggards

Consumers have long fretted about privacy and the security of their personal data. They have always demanded good service. But the connection between data and service was not something the mass of consumers thought much about. Until the current rash of data breaches, most people ignored the data they shared, clicking past all the internet terms-of-service pages without a second thought and imagining that the way their data was used didn't matter. But coverage of the Facebook/Cambridge Analytica data scandal and the advent of GDPR in Europe is creating an awareness of how much sensitive data is out there and how different companies are using it.

Companies who abuse consumer TRUST will pay the price in reduced profits.

Already, a majority of consumers we surveyed express concerns about data breaches, location tracking, and companies tracking their behavior as they visit sites across the internet. We expect an increase in people who share the perspective of the 45% of Fully Entitled consumers in our survey who agree with the statement, "It's shocking how bad companies are at knowing who I am or understanding my needs." We also expect an expansion of the 49% of consumers we surveyed who don't read all the messages even from companies they like, for the most part because "Most messages are about products and promotions that aren't relevant to me."

Consider the fate of the four consumer segments we introduced in chapter 1.

The Anticipators, 16% of all the consumers we surveyed, expect service in exchange for the data they share. They will become even more demanding as they learn the power of their data. They will be quite willing to share, but only with companies that deliver service based on that data. They will use GDPR and similar regulations to insist on the removal of their data from companies they consider to be behaving unhelpfully or exploitatively.

The Demanders, 23% of our survey sample, will become very transactional. The Millennials in this group, in particular, may begin to realize they can trade data for discounts. They'll become adept at tactics like abandoning online shopping carts in hope of getting a solicitation for a better deal. They will release their data only for the promise of value.

The Fully Entitled consumers, currently 30% of American and European consumers, will exhibit both of these behaviors. They will seek out and embrace companies with whom they can develop productive relationships—companies that use their data to deliver good service and act like trusted friends. And they will abandon companies who exploit their data for clueless messages and intrusive, irrelevant ads.

We expect all three of these segments to expand as data, and how marketers use it, becomes part of the national conversation in every developed nation. The rise of entitled and data-savvy consumers will make it impossible for companies to stay on the sidelines. They'll need consumer-first strategies for every type of entitled consumer.

If you fail to develop those strategies, you'll simply be left with the Indifferents. Currently 31% of consumers, this segment will shrink. Those that remain will be the oldest, least affluent, least active, least tech-savvy, and least engaged consumers. That's a risky customer base to stake your future on while your competitors develop a greater and greater ability to engage with and gain the loyalty of entitled consumers.

A shift in interactive interfaces will focus opportunities for marketers

The interactive world is not static. Twenty-five years ago, the web was born. Fifteen years ago, marketers' online efforts focused on websites and e-commerce. Ten years ago, social networking was hot. And in the past five years, mobile—and apps—have dominated the conversation. These new forms of interaction have not replaced their predecessors; we still use television ads, endcaps, and email to market, even in a mobile, social world. But the mix, the focus, and the investment priorities must shift to address new technologies.

Voice—and chat—are the new disruptive interfaces.

Smart speakers like Alexa and Google Home are fielding increasing numbers of web queries. Their alter egos on phones—Siri and Google Assistant, for example—are extending the trend.

The other element of this trend is chat. Tools like Facebook Messenger and Apple Business Chat now make it possible to ask free-form text questions of companies. And companies are putting chat interfaces on their customer support sites, with intelligent virtual agents behind them. Messaging platforms in China and elsewhere have already grown beyond communications and social interaction. WeChat, the most significant Asian platform, offers far-ranging functionality, including search and commerce, and has become the primary environment for interactions between consumers and brands.

What does this all add up to? It means that increasingly, consumers are going to start asking machines for answers, and the machines will reply.

The crucial shift here is a narrowing of access points. Google, Amazon/Alexa, and Apple/Siri determine which companies can connect with them and how. If you ask Alexa, "Where can I buy a good lawn mower?" the answer is going to be determined by the companies that Amazon allows access to that platform.

Similarly, messaging apps like Facebook Messenger and WhatsApp will play the same role, answering questions and even delivering products you request. They'll become crucial hubs for chat-based interactions, and they'll control which brands get access to their hubs.

The more people interact with these voice and chat portals, the more data the large technology companies operating these consumer platforms—Google, Amazon, Apple, and Facebook—will collect. They will use that data to deliver consumer-first service. And they will set the tone for the rest of marketing and customer service.

This means two things for brands.

First, brands must extend that relationship into these new customer platforms. If you were late to the web, you lost out. If you were late to mobile, you are losing out now. Once again, a platform shift is demanding your attention. Now is the time to determine how to add smart speakers and chat platforms to your mix of communications channels. Get good at this now, and you'll get a chance to respond to consumer queries in your market. Wait, and you may get shut out.

> In a world where chat hubs and smart speakers are increasingly important interfaces, a consumer-first relationship could **SAVE** your brand.

And second, now is the time to build as rich and helpful a direct consumer relationship as possible. When it's easiest to just ask Alexa, random brands will increasingly lose relevance. They'll also lose data because companies like Amazon, both online and with products like Alexa, will be building relationships by delivering brands' products. Brands that have cultivated a consumer-first marketing relationship—and the loyalty that comes from it—will be in the strongest position to continue to have relationships with consumers, even if they're also asking Alexa or Google to answer their product questions.

China will become the Darwinian laboratory for consumer-first marketing

Ironically, while the internet is bringing the world together, regional variations in the way it is regulated create dramatic differences in the way people perceive it.

These differences will create both challenges and opportunities for consumer-first marketers.

American lawmakers are reluctant to regulate the internet. Still, the litany of news about abuses and data breaches has created pressure to show that the government has its eye on protecting American consumers. As we write this, the winds of political change are sweeping across Congress. As a result, it's hard to know what kind of regulatory regime for data could eventually get enough backing to pass.

In the absence of regulatory stability, marketers are left to make judgments on how to use data. Using data purely to benefit consumers rarely has a drawback—this is why Amazon, Apple, Google, and Netflix haven't seen the scrutiny and PR backlash that Facebook has—yet. (Of these players, Amazon[2] and Google[3] could be at risk; we've already seen rumblings about whether they use data appropriately.)

Consumer-first marketers operating in the US are unlikely to go wrong if they provide transparency, collecting data that can help and using it in ways that an outside observer would find sensible, as we described in chapter 8. But any marketer must keep a close eye on potential data regulation that could create changes in how companies collect, protect, and use data and in how they send email, use mobile apps, and advertise.

In Europe, GDPR is the new focus of the regulatory regime, but the implementation of this regulation is still uncertain. It may, for example, interfere with companies' ability to advertise on media sites that use web-wide cookies. As a result, we think consumer-first marketing in Europe will be limited to direct relationships between companies and their customers. Handling data in such relationships is easier—getting consumer permission, data management, and even deleting data at the consumer's request is a more straightforward exercise without third parties.

The situation in China is far different. The social network WeChat and its mobile application have become a central part of how commerce happens. The government explicitly tracks consumers' social media use and has created a social credit system that actually rates residents on their citizenship.[4] Chinese citizens have more limited expectations about privacy; they know their data is out in the world and that companies, the government, and other people are looking at it, and there's very little they can do to control that.

A digital economy with few regulations on data creates the perfect conditions for consumer-first marketing. The next dozen

Indochinos will emerge at scale to serve a billion-and-a-half Chinese customers, using every bit of data available without restraint. The Chinese could become the ultimate entitled consumers, with the highest possible expectations for data use and personalized marketing to serve customer needs.

Chinese companies that master consumer-first marketing will rise quickly and scale up to become digital and real-world powerhouses. Those that do it poorly and exploitatively will rapidly get shamed and shunned. And the vast and powerful Chinese government will likely use the principles of consumer-first marketing to further nudge the behavior of its citizens in directions that the state believes will be most productive.

Consumer-first marketers in the rest of the world will find great examples of innovation—and cautionary tales—in China's no-holds-barred digital economy. And regulators and lawmakers in the US and Europe will look on carefully, perhaps bending regulations in the long term toward directions that will allow marketers to compete better in their regional economies.

Consumer-first marketing will give rise to a bespoke products economy

One of Indochino's advantages flows from its bespoke product cycle—you get the exact product you want, a product that exactly matches your preferences but didn't even exist until you asked for it. And it's not just Indochino. Amazon can now print any of millions of custom-published books for you on demand at the moment you ask for it. Tesla takes your order and then builds the customized car that matches it. Nike and Adidas even make shoes that match your desired colors and athletic needs.

There are two trends necessary to power this bespoke economy: consumer-first data and custom manufacturing.

Other data-focused businesses may embrace similar strategies. A toy retailer could rise to occupy the space left behind by Toys "R" Us' bankruptcy, 3-D printing new toys that match your kids' preferences and ages as they outgrow the plaything they're using now. Crate & Barrel could custom-manufacture housewares based on the colors and style of items you've bought in the past. HelloFresh, Blue Apron, Whole Foods, or Instacart could make and deliver meals to order that match your past buying patterns at the same time last year, last week, or the last time the Yankees were on a winning streak.

No matter what space you're in, keep an eye on the custom-manufacturing technologies that will be able to build the products you sell now. Your data stores are just the fuel you need to build a bespoke products business with your loyal customers.

Consumer-first principles will determine the rise of the next generation of technologies

The adoption cycle for new technologies follows a pattern. Startups innovate; leading-edge consumers or businesses try out their products. Some find them useful. They demand more features and lower prices, and the technology providers deliver, broadening the market. Finally, marketers begin to adopt the new technologies, helping to support them with advertising and marketing dollars.

This same cycle has repeated in areas as diverse as internet adoption, social media, mobile apps, and streaming media. But the cycle may change as consumers examine the technologies on the horizon in the 2020s.

Virtual reality (VR) right now is just a curiosity and a gaming platform. But it is a promising new way for customers to interact with brands. Brands like Indochino, Home Depot, or BMW could use it to leverage their knowledge of consumers to deliver fashion, home improvement, or driving experiences based on the preferences consumers have shared with them. The consumer-first marketers that use data to deliver personalized virtual experiences will win over early VR adopters; those who offer only generic, one-size-fits-all experiences will find their customers quickly bored.

Augmented reality (AR)—in which consumers use enhanced glasses or their smartphones to see virtual objects overlaid on their real-world vision—has great consumer-first potential as well. We think this will begin with store staff—like Indochino's Style Guides—whose glasses will allow them to know all about a consumer's preferences just by looking at her. We already described how Ikea lets you see what a couch would look like in your living room. As AR becomes more mainstream, stores will begin to provide virtual overlays for their real-world locations so that shoppers can see information displays about the products they're peering at, customized to their preferences. When Sophia has AR glasses, the products that fit her style will literally vibrate in her field of vision as she peruses the shelves.

As the internet spreads to all the devices in our homes, those devices will further deepen relationships with the companies that created them. Your Nest Thermostat will not only regulate your home's temperature but will tell Google when your family is most active, which in turn might determine how Google responds to search requests or decides what kind of entertainment is highlighted on the Chromecast. Your connected Samsung refrigerator will know all about your cooking and snacking habits and will help you create a shopping list; companies that make products that fit these preferences will vie to get their brand names onto that list. And your Tesla or Lincoln Navigator will make recommendations not just on what routes to take but on the local clubs and events where people who share your tastes are hanging out right now.

As for blockchain, the technology that underlies cryptocurrencies like Bitcoin, its future will impact every industry, including marketing. Most notably, it will impact how we think about identity. Blockchain will enable you to authenticate who you are in a foolproof way without cumbersome passwords or cookies. This will make it easier for consumers to control and share just the portions of their data that they believe will make marketers deliver better service—and to withdraw those permissions just as easily. This will reduce privacy concerns, enhance trust, and accelerate the adoption of consumer-first marketing, as it more quickly separates the helpful marketers from the loudmouthed boors.

WHAT'S NEXT FOR YOU?

The consumer-first future is coming. And as you can tell from the predictions in this chapter, its reach could be dramatic.

So what should you do about it? If you can't start the next Indochino, what can you do?

You can begin to prepare your company for that future.

The future that we see is one in which advancements in technology give brands the data and tools that allow them to build stronger, more friend-like relationships with consumers. Even as network television and print wane—and with them the power and reach of mass advertising—digital channels continue to give marketers the opportunity to create deeper engagement with individual consumers. That engagement will build on data and empathetic interactions.

In this future, for all the power that brands are able to consolidate, entitled consumers will be the ones demanding change. They will ask for more: more relevance, more value, more transparency, and more respect. They will demand communications—and ultimately bespoke products and services—that meet their needs, and they will look askance at generic messaging and one-size-fits-all products that don't work for them as individuals.

The race to the one-to-one future is on. Entitled consumers are driving, but the future is bright for marketers who are able to rise to their challenges.

Start transforming your approach by adopting the ideas in this book. Get started now. Or prepare to watch your competitors—some of which don't yet exist—pass you by.

THE CONSUMER-FIRST MARKETER'S TO-DO LIST

These are your to-dos to prepare your organization for consumer-first marketing:

- ☐ Prepare for a world of consumers whose unreasonable expectations are determined by their interactions with the most consumer-focused companies across all categories.

- ☐ Don't pollute the commons; look for ways to do more effective marketing with a lower volume of personalized marketing activity.

- ☐ Think more broadly about data; acquire the descriptive, social, relationship history, and situational data about your consumers that will position you to deliver the right interaction at the right moment.

- ☐ Embrace an omnichannel perspective, delivering an integrated experience in whatever channel a customer chooses to interact with, from websites to apps to email to in-person interactions.

- ☐ Deliver value in every marketing interaction by enhancing your product, reducing consumer effort, improving customer experience, and solving the customer's broader problem.

- ☐ Assemble the data and marketing techniques necessary to deliver the most relevant possible interaction for any given situation.

- ☐ Demonstrate respectful empathy by reducing message frequency and connecting in a way that is transparent to the consumer.

- ☐ Benchmark your consumer-first progress regularly by surveying your staff on all the dimensions of a consumer-first transformation.

- ☐ Learn from every engagement with the consumer. See each interaction more as an opportunity to listen than to speak.

- ☐ Begin the transformation now, taking small steps if necessary, to best prepare your company for a world where entitled consumers—and consumer-first marketers—have redefined what it means to compete.

ABOUT THE AUTHORS

NICK WORTH

Nick is a marketing expert whose varied career has given him unique insights into the ascendance of digital consumer engagement. He's worked in market research, board-level strategy, marketing technology, as a startup advisor, and, most notably, as a founder of one of the world's first and most successful digital agencies. With his partner, he took Schematic from a handful of people sitting at a booth in a Santa Monica coffee shop to 350 digital professionals serving some of the world's largest companies from six offices in three countries. Schematic brought the Olympics to the web as a live and on-demand experience for NBC, took the world's museums online for Google Art Project, and designed the UI of Sony's PS4, among many achievements. After WPP acquired Schematic, it became the foundation of the global digital agency POSSIBLE.

Currently the chief marketing officer of Selligent Marketing Cloud, Nick writes and speaks broadly about marketing, exploring the impact of technology advancements on marketing, how to engage Millennials, and the many challenges facing today's marketers. He has written for more than a dozen trade publications and has spoken at more than 50 marketing events in the US and across Europe.

Nick's other random achievements include groundbreaking voter education research prior to the first democratic elections in Mozambique and creating the first reliable public opinion polls in the Dominican Republic. His writing and production work for NBC at the 2002 Winter Olympic Games won an Emmy. He once alienated the entire city of Duluth, Minnesota, with an inflammatory article in his college newspaper. A graduate of Harvard College and Oxford University, Nick lives in London.

DAVE FRANKLAND

Dave is an independent writer, consultant, and thought leader. His research and opinions have been featured in media outlets from the *New York Times* and *Economist* to *Ad Age* and *1to1 Magazine*. His TV appearances include CNN's *The Situation Room*. He is a highly rated public speaker, having keynoted conferences around the world, and is equally comfortable addressing boardrooms and auditoriums.

Before the term Big Data existed, Dave saw the trend and cofounded the customer intelligence (CI) practice at Forrester Research. He and his team helped establish the CI role as one of Forrester's most successful practices. He has helped executives at hundreds of companies to define their customer relationship strategy and has worked directly with many of the companies whose case studies are featured in this book.

Previously, Dave served as the chief strategy officer at Selligent, as well as in various roles at DoubleClick (acquired by Google), NRW, and Hill & Knowlton. He grew up in Dublin, Ireland, and holds degrees from the National University of Ireland, Galway; Trinity College Dublin; and the University of Stirling in Scotland. He lives in Florida with his wife and two children.

JOSH BERNOFF

Josh Bernoff is a bestselling author and recognized expert on writing, editing, and analytical thinking. His most recent book is *Writing Without Bullshit: Boost Your Career by Saying What You Mean* (HarperBusiness, 2016). The *Globe and Mail* called it "a Strunk & White for the modern knowledge worker."

His first book, *Groundswell: Winning in a World Transformed by Social Technologies* (Harvard Business Press, 2008), written with Charlene Li, was a *BusinessWeek* bestseller. Abbey Klaassen, the editor of *Advertising Age*, picked it as "the best book ever written on marketing and media." He also cowrote *Empowered: Unleash Your Employees, Energize Your Customers, Transform Your Business* (HBR Press, 2010), with Ted Schadler, and *The Mobile Mind Shift: Engineer Your Business to Win in the Mobile Moment* (Groundswell Press, 2014), with Ted Schadler and Julie Ask.

For 20 years Josh was a principal analyst and senior vice president, idea development at Forrester Research, the elite technology research company. In that position he wrote over 100 reports, gave speeches all over the world, and worked with Fortune 500 clients on business strategy. He appeared on *60 Minutes* and got quoted everywhere from the *Wall Street Journal* to *TV Guide*. The Society for New Communications Research recognized him as "Visionary of the Year."

He lives in the Boston area with his wife and two children, who are in college. He is the volunteer CEO of a nonprofit, wellnesscampaign.org, dedicated to the pursuit of wellness through changing habits.

Josh blogs every weekday at bernoff.com.

RESEARCH METHODOLOGY

The Entitled Consumer Survey, which forms the basis for the consumer entitlement segments, is an online survey of 7,000 consumers carried out by Research Now SSI between August 24 and September 27, 2017. Respondents are based in the following countries: France (1,000), Germany (1,000), Italy, (1,000), Spain (1,000), the UK (1,000), and the US (2,000).

The sample consists of 51.6% female and 48.2% male respondents. The average age of respondents is 47 years old, and respondents included Millennials (aged 18–34 comprising 26.6% of the sample), Gen Xers (aged 35–54 comprising 36.6% of the sample), and Baby Boomers (aged 55 plus comprising 36.8% of the sample). The survey respondents were randomly selected from Research Now SSI's proprietary panel.

The Entitlement Factor was derived using data-reductive, latent factor analytics, yielding a multi-item "Entitlement Scale" with a high degree of Reliability (alpha > 0.8) and predictive utility that was consistent across age bands and market. Comparisons using the Entitlement factor were all conducted using a conventional significance criteria (p. <= .05).

The authors, Research Now SSI, and Econsultancy worked closely together on designing the survey and extracting the key theme. Data analysis was conducted by KGR+C, a strategic research, insights, and analytics consultancy.

Qualitative research includes interviews with marketers and experts, both in person and via phone calls. The authors also moderated four live discussion focus group interviews with consumers between September 2017 and February 2018 in Austin, Texas; London, UK; Munich, Germany; and Stockholm, Sweden. The interviews each included six to ten participants who were unknown to the moderators in advance of the interviews.

ACKNOWLEDGMENTS

One morning, in Lisbon, Portugal, we were sitting beside each other listening to an author talk about marketing effectiveness at a client conference. His presentation connected with the entire audience. We could almost hear minds opening and gears turning as an audience of professionals listened, learned, and started to think differently about a new and exciting approach to their work. Something clicked inside the two of us, and we looked at each other—almost in sync—and said, "We need to write a book." We had been in a months-long discussion about why forming durable connections with consumers was so hard, but it wasn't until that moment that we realized that we wanted to formalize our thinking and contribute something to the debate. Three years later and with a lot of help from an army of supporters, we're ready to put our ideas out there. Our hope is that we can connect with our readers as powerfully as that speaker did, sparking much needed change in how marketers engage with customers.

Our ideas come from our experiences working with marketers and experts, and we are extremely grateful to the friends, colleagues, and clients who have inspired, challenged, and shaped so many of our ideas. We are especially indebted to all the people on the front lines of consumer-first marketing who generously shared their stories and agreed to be profiled in the book, even those who asked us to keep them anonymous.

Friends and colleagues around the world assisted in ways big and small. We want to thank John Hernandez and the Selligent Marketing Cloud executive team, past and present, for their steadfast support of this effort. Todd McCaslin, Kat Berman, Jan Teerlinck, April Mullen, and all the other Selligent thought leaders made essential contributions. We also offer a separate thanks to April and her crew at "Women of Email" for their unfiltered perspective on what's happening in the corporate world of email. We're indebted to Alex Handcock, Nina Maurus, and Georg Loewen for corralling the Munich focus group and all their other support, and Ragna Lundström for the smörgåsbord of insights from her Stockholm focus group. We extend a special thanks to Nikki Reyes, who provided invaluable research support, and Carly Fordyce for her administrative pertinacity. And we'd like to express our sincere appreciation for Emily Riley, whose insightful commentary and research helped shape our ideas, analysis, and recommendations throughout the entire project.

When we approached Steve Young about writing the foreword, he was typically magnanimous. It's not every day that an NFL Hall of Fame quarterback has got your back, and we are extremely grateful for his thoughtful insights and analogy tying together his two—highly successful—careers.

A big thanks goes to Naren Aryal, Kristin Perry, and the team at Mascot Books for their constant encouragement and enthusiasm and for turning our manuscript into a beautiful book. We'd also like to recognize Kate Schomaker for her expert copyediting. Others who contributed to the final product, and to whom we want to express our sincere appreciation, include Stephani Finks for a beautiful and striking cover, Vladimir Mirkovic at Transart Design for the interior graphics, the team at SSI for its flawless survey execution, and Ben Kim-Gervey, Ph.D. at KGR+C for analyzing our consumer research across six countries.

We owe a particular debt of gratitude to Josh Bernoff, whose contribution cannot be overstated—or sufficiently acknowledged. When we first reached out to Josh, he freely gave his advice and input. Once he climbed on board the project, he continuously delivered on his billing as the "book whisperer." He challenged and shaped our ideas, project-managed our production process (we're sorry!), and helped bring our ideas to life in engaging prose.

Finally, and most importantly, we'd like to thank our families for putting up with us before, during, and after the writing of this book.

Our hope is that we encourage marketers to change how they build relationships with entitled consumers. We look forward to continuing that dialog at www.entitledconsumer.com.

—Nick Worth and Dave Frankland
London, England, and Palm Beach, Florida

ENDNOTES

CHAPTER 1

1. If you're a nervous flyer, you could always use the eaze app (eaze.com). They deliver marijuana right to your door.

2. In major cities, the average wait time for an Uber is three minutes. "Uber CEO explains why Arrival Time on the app is never accurate" by Yoni Heisler, BGR, January 4, 2016. See http://bgr.com/2016/01/04/uber-arrival-time-late/.

3. Richard White of UserVoice was among the first to recognize the importance of entitled consumers. See "The Era of the Entitled Consumer and the Future of Customer Engagement," by Richard White, July 22, 2014, on the UserVoice Product Management blog. See https://community.uservoice.com/blog/the-era-of-the-entitled-customer-and-the-future-of-customer-engagement/.

4. While Samsung refrigerators don't order food for you yet, you can use a touch-sensitive interactive display on some models to order food right from the refrigerator. "MasterCard, Samsung Make Everyday Shopping Easier in Tomorrow's Smart Home with Launch of Groceries by MasterCard App," (press release), January 5, 2016. See https://newsroom.mastercard.com/press-releases/mastercard-samsung-make-everyday-shopping-easier-in-tomorrows-smart-home-with-launch-of-groceries-by-mastercard-app/.

5. Key results from the Temkin Group study are in "The (Large) Connection Between Emotion and Loyalty," by Bruce Temkin, August 22, 2016, in Customer Experience Matters. See https://experiencematters.blog/2016/08/22/the-large-connection-between-emotion-and-loyalty/.

6. The Lithium study is reported in "Number of Bad Experiences that Would Cause US and UK Internet Users to Stop Using/Switch Brands, by Product/Service Category, Dec 2016 (% of respondents)" March 29, 2017, in eMarketer. See http://www.emarketer.com/Chart/Number-of-Bad-Experiences-that-Would-Cause-US-UK-Internet-Users-Stop-UsingSwitch-Brands-by-ProductService-Category-Dec-2016-of-respondents/206097.

CHAPTER 2

1. Tragedy of the commons story from "The Tragedy of the Commons" by Garett Hardin, December 13, 1968, in *Science*. See http://science.sciencemag.org/content/162/3859/1243.full.

2. Yankelovich study cited in "Anywhere the Eye Can See, It's Likely to See an Ad," by Louise Story, January 15, 2007, in the *New York Times*. See https://www.nytimes.com/2007/01/15/business/media/15everywhere.html.

3. "Towards a Bra-free Instagram Experience" by Lauren Hallden, December 30, 2017, in *NewCo Shift* on Medium. See https://shift.newco.co/towards-a-bra-free-instagram-experience-3e43273b611f.

4. Edward Papazian quoted in "Advertisers At Risk Of Consumer Burnout," by Laurie Sullivan, January 16, 2017, in *MediaPost*. See https://www.mediapost.com/publications/article/292938/.

5. Statistics from figure 2 in the Forrester Report "The End Of Advertising As We Know It," by James L. McQuivey and Keith Johnston, May 2, 2017. See https://www.forrester.com/report/The+End+Of+Advertising+As+We+Know+It/-/E-RES137501. Full access restricted to clients of Forrester Research.

6. Clickthrough rates from "Average display advertising clickthrough rates," by Dave Chaffey, March 14, 2018, in *Smart Insights*. See https://www.smartinsights.com/internet-advertising/internet-advertising-analytics/display-advertising-clickthrough-rates/.

7. Banner ad accidental click rate from mobile location firm Retale, cited in "60% Of All Mobile Banner Ad Clicks Are Accidents," by Ben Frederick, February 5, 2016, in MoBlog on *MediaPost*. See https://www.mediapost.com/publications/article/268266/60-of-all-mobile-banner-ad-clicks-are-accidents.html.

8. Ad intrusiveness survey statistics from a survey of 1,055 online browsers in the US, UK, Germany, and France in the HubSpot AdBlock Plus Research Survey, Q2 2016. Published in "Majority agree ads are more intrusive today," July 13, 2016, in *HubSpot Research*. See https://research.hubspot.com/charts/majority-agree-ads-are-more-intrusive-today.

9. Google plans for blocking autoplay from "Chrome will get better at stopping those annoying autoplay videos," by Thuy Ong, September 15, 2017, in *The Verge*. See https://www.theverge.com/2017/9/15/16311310/google-chrome-autoplay-videos-january.

10. Statistics cited here come from the Inbox Marketer 2017 North American Email Benchmark & Trends Report. See https://cdn2.hubspot.net/hubfs/487979/Live_Resource_Files/2017%20North%20American%20Email%20Benchmarks%20&%20Trends%20Report.pdf.

11. Dela Quist quotes from "More Emails, More Sales? The Surprising Argument For Aggressive Email Marketing," by Lissa Harris, October 2, 2017, in *Entrepreneur Magazine*. See https://www.entrepreneur.com/article/299600.

12. Email statistics from HubSpot and Litmus' "Science of Email 2014" report, by Dan Zarrella. See https://offers.hubspot.com/science-of-email-marketing-2014-report.

13. Multitasking statistic from *Generation M2 : Media in the Lives of 8- to 18-Year-Olds*, by Victoria J. Rideout, Ulla G. Foehr, and Donald F. Roberts, Kaiser Family Foundation, January 2010, p. 33. See https://kaiserfamilyfoundation.files.wordpress.com/2013/04/8010.pdf.

14. Texting while driving statistic from "People Who Text and Drive Are Jacking Up Your Insurance Premiums," by Brad Tuttle, March 20, 2017, in *Money*. See http://time.com/money/4706657/auto-insurance-rates-distracted-driving-smartphones/.

15. Quote from "The New Creative Paradigm Part 1: Understanding New Consumer Behavior Patterns," by John Nardone, June 30, 2017, p. 3. See http://www.flashtalking.com/new-creative-paradigm-white-paper-request/.

16. Statistics from observation of 2,400 viewers shown in "What Drives Engagement and Recall in Ad Delivery?" by Council for Research Excellence, January 31, 2017, p. 34. See http://www.researchexcellence.com/files/pdf/2017-02/id414_cre_hub_presentation_for_media_insights_conference_01312017.pdf.

17. Definition from *Outside In: The Power of Putting Customers at the Center of your Business*, by Harley Manning and Kerry Bodine (New Harvest, 2012), p. 7.

18. Stock performance from "The 2105 Customer Experience ROI Study: Demonstrating the business value of a great customer experience," by Jon Picoult, Watermark Consulting, p. 4. See https://www.watermarkconsult.net/docs/Watermark-Customer-Experience-ROI-Study.pdf.

19. Revenue growth statistics are based on compound annual growth rates from 2010 to 2015. Source of results is US Securities and Exchange Commission Filings. Based on from figure 1 in the Forrester Report "The CX Transformation Imperative: It's Not Whether To Transform CX; It's When And How" by Harley Manning, September 14, 2016. See https://www.forrester.com/report/The+CX+Transformation+Imperative/-/E-RES134662. Full access restricted to clients of Forrester Research.
20. Quote from "Four Ways Marketers Can Stop Damaging Their Profession," by Augie Ray, September 15, 2016, on the Gartner for Marketers blog. See https://blogs.gartner.com/augie-ray/2016/09/15/four-ways-marketers-can-stop-damaging-their-profession/.

CHAPTER 3

1. For the original research, see "Consumers and their Brands: Understanding Relationship Theory in Consumer Research," by Susan Fournier, 1998, *Journal of Consumer Research*, 24 (4), 343–373. See https://academic.oup.com/jcr/article-abstract/24/4/343/1797962.
2. From "Unlock the Mysteries of Your Customer Relationships," by Jill Avery, Susan Fournier, and John Wittenbraker, July–August 2014, *Harvard Business Review*. See https://hbr.org/2014/07/unlock-the-mysteries-of-your-customer-relationships.
3. Statistics from "State of the Connected Consumer," by Salesforce, p. 46. See https://a.sfdcstatic.com/content/dam/www/ocms-backup/assets/pdf/misc/socc-2016.pdf.
4. Statistics from "Quarterly Digital Intelligence Briefing: The Multichannel Reality," by Econsultancy, September 2015. See https://econsultancy.com/reports/the-multichannel-reality. Available to subscribers only.
5. Quote from "Cringe-Worthy Attempts to Market to Millennials," by Albizu Garcia, *ADWEEK*, August 18, 2017. See http://www.adweek.com/digital/albizu-garcia-gain-guest-post-cringe-worthy-attempts-to-market-to-Millennials/.
6. Statistics from "The Digital Universe of Opportunities: Rich Data and the Increasing Value of the Internet of Things," by Vernon Turner, April 2014, IDC iView, sponsored by EMC. See https://www.emc.com/leadership/digital-universe/2014iview/executive-summary.htm.
7. Quote from *Age of Context* by Robert Scoble and Shel Israel (CreateSpace, 2013), p. 42.
8. Statistic from "The Personalization Imperative for Content Marketing," by Michael Brenner, Marketing Insider Group, December 2016, p. 4. See https://pages.onespot.com/rs/745-SIY-586/images/OS-ContentPersonalization-FinalRGB-10MB.pdf.
9. Statistics from "State of the Connected Consumer," by Salesforce, p. 23. See https://a.sfdcstatic.com/content/dam/www/ocms-backup/assets/pdf/misc/socc-2016.pdf.
10. Statistic from "OMNI-CHANNEL MARKETING 101: Bridging the Gap Between Online and Offline - How to align your marketing to today's omni-channel consumer journey," by Angela Sanfilippo, AgileOne, April 2, 2015. See http://blog.agilone.com/bridging-the-gap-between-online-and-offline-how-to-align-your-marketing-to-todays-omni-channel-consumer-journey.
11. Statistic from "Prescription for Cutting Costs," by Fred Reichheld, Bain & Company, p. 1. See http://www.bain.com/Images/BB_Prescription_cutting_costs.pdf.

12. Statistic from "Personalization Sees Payoffs in Marketing Emails," January 28, 2014, *eMarketer*. See https://www.emarketer.com/Article/Personalization-Sees-Payoffs-Marketing-Emails/1010563.

13. From "The CMO Solution Guide: Context and Consumers," by The CMO Club in partnership with Selligent, p. 16. See http://www.selligent.com/resources/white-papers/the-cmo-solution-guide-context-and-consumers/wpcmous.

CHAPTER 4

1. Boston Consulting Group's perspective on personalization appears in "Profiting from Personalization," by Mark Abraham, Steve Mitchelmore, Sean Collins, Jeff Maness, Mark Kistulinec, Shervin Khodabandeh, Daniel Hoenig, and Jody Visser, May 8, 2017, in BCG. See https://www.bcg.com/publications/2017/retail-marketing-sales-profiting-personalization.aspx.

2. Example described in "5 Killer Examples of Data-Driven Marketing," by Ritika Puri, December 19, 2017, on the Wordstream blog. See https://www.wordstream.com/blog/ws/2016/08/25/data-driven-marketing.

3. For more detail on Stitch Fix and other companies collecting body measurements, read "Companies race to gather a newly prized currency: Our body measurements," by Drew Harwell, January 16, 2018, *Washington Post*. See https://www.washingtonpost.com/business/economy/companies-race-to-gather-a-newly-prized-currency-our-body-measurements/2018/01/16/5af28d98-f6e8-11e7-beb6-c8d48830c54d_story.html.

4. Read about the Axe Brazil story in "Axe Remakes Story of Romeo—100,000 Times," by Jack Neff, August 10, 2015, *Ad Age*. See http://adage.com/article/see-the-spot/unilever-s-axe-remakes-story-romeo-100-000-times/299888/.

5. Read about Doggyloot's emails in "Are You Embracing Personalization in Marketing?" by Liz Froment, February 12, 2016, Zembula. See https://www.zembula.com/blog/embracing-personalization-marketing/.

6. Read about Cadbury's personalized marketing in "Cadbury Boosts New Products with Personalized Video," by Alarice Rajogopal, February 25, 2015, *Consumer Goods Technology*. See https://consumergoods.com/cadbury-boosts-new-products-personalized-video.

7. Read about Paper Style's strategy in "MarketingSherpa Email Summit 2013: Using buyer behavior in email campaigns," by David Kirkpatrick, February 21, 2013, on the MarketingSherpa blog. See https://sherpablog.marketingsherpa.com/email-marketing/buyer-behavior-email-campaigns/.

8. For more on the Accenture study, see "Consumers Welcome Personalized Offerings but Businesses Are Struggling to Deliver, Finds Accenture Interactive Personalization Research" (press release) by Accenture, October 13, 2016. See https://newsroom.accenture.com/news/consumers-welcome-personalized-offerings-but-businesses-are-struggling-to-deliver-finds-accenture-interactive-personalization-research.htm.

9. Read the Secure Retirements case in "Smart Content Case Study: Hyper-Personalized Newsletters," by Donna Arriaga, May 26, 2016, on the Denamico blog. See http://blog.denamico.com/smart-content-case-study-hyper-personalized-newsletters.
10. Based on Wyanoke presentation at the Selligent Consumer-First Summit, February 2018.
11. Electronic Arts reveals its strategy in "A Sneak Peek into Data and Electronic Arts," by Navid Aghdaie, September 2015, in CERN Root Data Analysis Framework. See https://indico.cern.ch/event/349459/contributions/822815/attachments/1157864/1665557/Navid.Aghdaie.CERN.ROOT20.final.pdf.
12. Read about EA's player database in "Data Lets Electronic Arts Put Players First," by Beth Negus Viveiros, May 25, 2017, in *Chief Marketer*. See http://www.chiefmarketer.com/data-lets-electronic-arts-put-players-first/.
13. Read about the Merci app in "STM: Interacting with 1.2 Million Commuters Every Day," by Elisabeth Peternek, June 18, 2014, from SAP. See https://news.sap.com/stm-interacting-with-million-commuters/.
14. Metro magazine describes the Montreal STM app offers in "Montreal transit app rewards riders with personalized offers," by Nicole Schlosser, November 18, 2013, in *Metro*. See http://www.metro-magazine.com/management-operations/article/211834/montreal-transit-app-rewards-riders-with-personalized-offers.
15. For more on the marketing program at STM, read the profile "Pierre Bourbonniere, La Société de transport de Montréal (STM)" at Constellation Research. See https://www.constellationr.com/pierre-bourbonniere-la-soci-t-de-transport-de-montr-al-stm.
16. For more on airline personalization, read "Airlines Personalize the Passenger Experience With New Apps and Devices," by Justin Backman, Bloomberg, November 16, 2017, in Skift. See https://skift.com/2017/11/16/airlines-personalize-the-passenger-experience-with-new-apps-and-devices/.
17. The EasyJet personalized marketing story appears in "How EasyJet Transformed Customer Data into Emotional Anniversary Stories," January 9, 2017, in Think. See https://and-think.com/2017/01/09/how-easyjet-transformed-customer-data-into-emotional-anniversary-stories/.
18. The Global Giving case study is in "Email Marketing: Charity crowdfunding website sees 10x increase in engagement from personalized email," by Courtney Eckerle, September 28, 2016, in MarketingSherpa. See https://www.marketingsherpa.com/article/case-study/globalgiving-personalized-email.
19. The full and fascinating story of the Disney Magic Band is in "Disney's $1 Billion Bet on a Magical Wristband," by Cliff Kuang, March 10, 2015, in *Wired*. See https://www.wired.com/2015/03/disney-magicband/.
20. More on Disney customer experience technology is in "Disney Uses Big Data, IoT And Machine Learning To Boost Customer Experience," by Bernard Marr, August 24, 2017, in *Forbes* contributor blogs. See https://www.forbes.com/sites/bernardmarr/2017/08/24/disney-uses-big-data-iot-and-machine-learning-to-boost-customer-experience/#1ec50c293387.
21. We heard about Emirates and how its first-class bartenders share information at a Forrester Forum in Europe.
22. Read all about Coolblue in "Coolblue Case Study" in Selligent. See http://www.selligent.com/sites/default/files/media/case-study-coolblue-us.pdf.

23. A description of John Deere's data-driven strategy is in "John Deere Is Revolutionizing Farming With Big Data," by Mark van Rijmenam, February 20, 2015, in Datafloq. See https://datafloq.com/read/john-deere-revolutionizing-farming-big-data/511.

CHAPTER 5

1. For more on journey maps, read "Using Customer Journey Maps to Improve Customer Experience," by Adam Richardson, November 15, 2010, HBR online. See https://hbr.org/2010/11/using-customer-journey-maps-to.
2. The Barclays Africa story is in the Forrester report "Use Customer Journey Mapping to Make Your Culture Customer-Obsessed," by Joana van den Brink-Quintanilha and Samuel Stern, August 11, 2016. See https://www.forrester.com/report/Use+Customer+Journey+Mapping+To+Make+Your+Culture+CustomerObsessed/-/E-RES123364. Access restricted to Forrester clients only.
3. Statistic from the Forrester report "The State of Customer Journey Mapping, 2017" by Joana van den Brink-Quintanilha and Tony Costa, August 23, 2107. See https://www.forrester.com/report/The+State+Of+Customer+Journey+Mapping+2017/-/E-RES137977. Access restricted to Forrester clients only.
4. Quote from "The End of the Customer Journey" on the Retention Science blog. See https://www.retentionscience.com/blog/the-end-of-the-customer-journey/.
5. Statistic from "To understand customers, first you need to understand their Device Graphs," by Barry Levine July 17, 2017, MarTech Today. See https://martechtoday.com/understand-customers-first-need-understand-devices-201065.
6. Neiman Marcus and Crate & Barrel stories from "10 Examples of Outstanding Multichannel Brands," by Dan Virgillito on Shopifyplus, October 2, 2017, on MarTech Today. See https://www.shopify.com/enterprise/10-examples-of-outstanding-omnichannel-brands.
7. Value City Furniture story from "Value City Furniture Increases Shopping Cart Abandonment Revenue by 283%," by Maria Page, July 8, 2015, on the SmarterHQ blog. See https://smarterhq.com/blog/value-city-furniture-increases-shopping-cart-abandonment-revenue-by-283.
8. Fabletics story from "'Brick mining': Why a need for data led Fabletics to open stores," by Laura Heller, June 9, 2017, in RetailDive. See https://www.retaildive.com/news/brick-mining-why-a-need-for-data-led-fabletics-to-open-stores/444662/.
9. TBC Bank story from "FICO Decisions Awards 2016: Customer Onboarding & Management," December 21, 2016, on the FICO blog. See http://www.fico.com/en/blogs/marketing-customer-engagement/tbc-bank-wins-award-for-omni-channel-customer-engagement/.
10. AI statistics from "10 Ways Machine Learning Is Revolutionizing Marketing," by Louis Columbus, February 5, 2018, in Forbes online. See https://www.forbes.com/sites/louiscolumbus/2018/02/25/10-ways-machine-learning-is-revolutionizing-marketing/#27a0c28b5bb6.

CHAPTER 6

1. Quotes from "The T-Mobile CEO who calls his competition 'dumb and dumber' explains how he doubled customers in 4 years, and how a group of employees made him cry," by Richard Feloni, October 7, 2016, *Business Insider*. See http://www.businessinsider.com/t-mobile-ceo-john-legere-interview-2016-10.
2. Market share information from "US Wireless Market to Add 100 Million Subscribers by 2020 says Strategy Analytics," by Susan Welsh de Grimaldo (press release), June 30, 2015, Strategy Analytics. See https://www.strategyanalytics.com/strategy-analytics/news/strategy-analytics-press-releases/strategy-analytics-press-release/2015/06/30/us-wireless-market-to-add-100-million-subscribers-by-2020-says-strategy-analytics#.Wu9DQtMvxo5.
3. Just as we were writing this, T-Mobile announced plans to take over and merge with fourth-place US mobile operator Sprint, a company whose position had been weakened by T-Mobile's surge in growth.
4. Subscriber statistics from "T-Mobile: Q4 strong, but can Un-carrier mojo last forever?" by Larry Dignan, February 8, 2018, *ZDNet*. See https://www.zdnet.com/article/t-mobile-q4-strong-but-can-un-carrier-mojo-last-forever/.
5. Zappos information from "Competitive Spirit, Black Monday and Promotional Discounts Give Rise to a Merry Online Retail Season," by Marianne Bickle, November 30, 2010, in *Forbes* online. See https://www.forbes.com/sites/prospernow/2010/11/30/competitive-spirit-black-monday-and-promotional-discounts-give-rise-to-a-merry-online-retail-season/#1f0754135b1d.
6. USAA Customer Experience Ratings from "Regions and Citizens Earn Top Customer Experience Ratings for Banks," by Bruce Temkin, March 22, 2017, on Customer Experience Matters. See https://experiencematters.blog/2017/03/22/regions-and-citizens-earn-top-customer-experience-ratings-for-banks/#more-31800.
7. USAA information from "USAA Rolls Out Conversational Alexa Skill Using Clinc AI," by Grace Noto, August 2, 2017, *Bank Innovation*. See https://bankinnovation.net/2017/08/usaa-rolls-out-conversational-alexa-skill-using-clinc-ai/.
8. USAA information from "USAA Offering No-Interest Payroll Advance Loans to Military Members During Shutdown," by KENS 5 staff, January 21, 2018, on WLTX19. See https://www.wltx.com/article/news/nation/usaa-offering-no-interest-payroll-advance-loans-to-military-members-during-shutdown/101-509960173.
9. UK holiday promotions described in "How four UK retailers are giving consumers the 'VIP' treatment this Christmas," by Nikki Gilliland, November 22, 2016, Econsultancy. See https://econsultancy.com/blog/68540-how-four-uk-retailers-are-giving-consumers-the-vip-treatment-this-christmas/.
10. Carnival Cruise information from "Carnival's New Internet Speeds Blow Away Land Based Connections," by Ben Souza, February 26, 2018, on CruiseFever. See https://cruisefever.net/carnivals-new-internet-speeds-blow-away-land-based-connections/.
11. This analysis of mobile strategy comes from the book *The Mobile Mind Shift: Engineer Your Business to Win in the Mobile Moment* by Ted Schadler, Josh Bernoff, and Julie Ask (Groundswell Press, 2014).
12. IKEA app described in "So Smart: New IKEA App Places Virtual Furniture in Your Home," by Liz Stinson, August 20, 2013, *Wired*. See https://www.wired.com/2013/08/a-new-ikea-app-lets-you-place-3d-furniture-in-your-home/.

13. GiffGaff statistic from "The digitisation of everything," by Ernst & Young, p. 12. See http://www.ey.com/Publication/vwLUAssets/The_digitisation_of_everything_-_How_organisations_must_adapt_to_changing_consumer_behaviour/$FILE/EY_Digitisation_of_everything.pdf.

14. This description of customer experience comes from *Outside In: The Power of Putting the Customer at the Center of Your Business,*" by Harley Manning and Kerry Bodine (New Harvest, 2012).

15. Details on Surefoot program from "Growing Pains Program," on Surefoot site. See http://www.surefoot.com/children_skiboots.php.

16. You can read the Darn Tough socks warranty at https://darntough.com/pages/our-guarantee.

17. Sephora information from "30 minutes with Sephora's head of marketing," by Cara Salpini, November 29, 2017, on RetailDive. See https://www.retaildive.com/news/30-minutes-with-sephoras-head-of-marketing/510300/.

18. Tesla service statistic from "Tesla Expanding Service Network Ahead Of Model 3 Launch," by Steve Hanley, July 12, 2017, on CleanTechnica. See https://cleantechnica.com/2017/07/12/tesla-expanding-service-network-ahead-model-3-launch/.

19. Statistics from Forrester report "The Values-Based Consumer," by Anjali Lai, April 6, 2017. See https://www.forrester.com/report/The+ValuesBased+Consumer/-/E-RES137665. Accessible to Forrester clients only.

20. See the Forrester report "Align With Consumers' Values To Win Their Hearts And Wallets," by Jim Mail and Henry Peyret, April 6, 2017. See https://www.forrester.com/report/Align+With+Consumers+Values+To+Win+Their+Hearts+And+Wallets/-/E-RES136198. Accessible to Forrester clients only.

21. TOMS Shoes information from "Is TOMS Shoes Listening to Its Critics," by Joshua Keating, October 17, 2013, *Slate*. See http://www.slate.com/blogs/the_world_/2013/10/17/toms_shoes_to_begin_producing_shoes_in_haiti_will_this_be_a_more_effective.html.

22. Novo Nordisk information from "The World's Top 25 For-Benefit Companies," by Rachel Zurer, November 6, 2016, on Conscious Company Media. See https://consciouscompanymedia.com/sustainable-business/the-worlds-top-25-for-benefit-companies/.

23. Newman's Own financials from "Newman's Own Foundation Reaches Milestone of $500 Million to Charity," (press release), February 1, 2018, on Newsman's Own Foundation website. See http://newmansownfoundation.org/news/newman-s-own-foundation-reaches-milestone-of-500-million-to-charity/.

24. Ecosia announced that it had planted 25 million trees in a tweet. See https://twitter.com/Ecosia/status/991604467828174848.

25. Hyatt information from "Hyatt's Random Acts of Generosity," by Rob Walker, June 17, 2009, *New York Times Magazine*. See https://www.nytimes.com/2009/06/21/magazine/21FOB-Consumed-t.html?_r=0.

26. Disney information from "Disney World Security Guard Asks Little Princess For Her Autograph (PHOTO)," by Jessica Samakow July 23, 2012, on *HuffPost*. See https://www.huffingtonpost.com/2012/07/23/disney-world-security-guard_n_1695034.html.

27. Rackspace information from "The Value in Wowing Your Customers," by Fred Reichheld, March 13, 2012, *Harvard Business Review*. See https://hbr.org/2012/03/the-value-in-wowing-your-customers.
28. Zappos values from "Zappos 10 Core Values" on the Zappos Insights site. See https://www.zapposinsights.com/about/core-values.
29. Zappos information from "Zappos Sends You Flowers," by Meg Marco, October 16, 2017, on Consumerist. See https://consumerist.com/2007/10/16/zappos-sends-you-flowers/.
30. Google describes micro-moments in detail at "Micro-Moments" on the Think With Google site. See https://www.thinkwithgoogle.com/marketing-resources/micro-moments/.

CHAPTER 7

1. Thomas Rubens is a composite of typical Kinepolis customers.
2. Statistics from "The 2017 State of Personalization Report" by Segment, pp. 3, 7. See http://grow.segment.com/Segment-2017-Personalization-Report.pdf.

CHAPTER 8

1. Uber's tweet is at https://twitter.com/Uber_Comms/status/975776694857474048.
2. Fatemeh Khatibloo's quote appears in "Privacy Is An Opportunity, Not A Burden," by Allison Schiff, April 27, 2016, in *AdExchanger*. See https://adexchanger.com/data-exchanges/privacy-opportunity-not-burden/.
3. Cost of data breach from "2017 Ponemon Cost of Data Breach Study," by Ponemon Institute. See https://www.ibm.com/security/data-breach.
4. More detail at open data frameworks is at "Examining the Open Data Movement," by Kelsey Finch, January 25, 2018, on Future of Privacy Forum. See https://fpf.org/2018/01/25/examining-the-open-data-movement/.
5. More on Bed Bath & Beyond's problems is in "One reason why Bed Bath & Beyond has problems competing—stores are 'a mess,'" by Tonya Garci, April 16, 2018, in *MarketWatch*. See https://www.marketwatch.com/story/one-reason-why-bed-bath-beyond-has-problems-competingstores-are-a-mess-2018-04-12.
6. Zeynep Tufekci's comprehensive analysis of Facebook's history of problems is in "Why Zuckerberg's 14-Year Apology Tour Hasn't Fixed Facebook," by Zeynep Tufekci, April 6, 2018, *Wired*. See https://www.wired.com/story/why-zuckerberg-15-year-apology-tour-hasnt-fixed-facebook/.
7. *Wired* describes its approach in "How Wired Is Going To Handle Ad Blocking," February 8, 2016, *Wired*. See https://www.wired.com/how-wired-is-going-to-handle-ad-blocking/.

8. See the Forrester report "Brief: Be Cool, Not Creepy," by Fatemeh Khatibloo, January 29, 2016. See https://www.forrester.com/report/Brief+Be+Cool+Not+Creepy/-/E-RES131441.

9. Microsoft describes its research in "Microsoft Research reveals understanding gap in the brand-consumer data exchange," June 3, 2015, in Microsoft Asia News Center. See https://news.microsoft.com/apac/2015/06/03/microsoft-research-reveals-understanding-gap-in-the-brand-consumer-data-exchange/.

10. MarketingSherpa data on unsubscribes comes from "MarketingSherpa Customer Satisfaction Research Study," on MarketingSherpa. See https://www.marketingsherpa.com/freestuff/customer-first-study#report.

11. SendGrid data on email unsubscribe rates from "Fighting Email Fatigue: When is Your Email Frequency Too High?" by Jillian Wohlfarth, June 27, 2017, on the SendGrid blog. See https://sendgrid.com/blog/fighting-email-fatigue-when-is-your-email-frequency-too-high/.

12. More detail on the RBC experience is in "The Quest for Customer Focus," by Ranjay Gulati and James B. Oldroyd, April 2005, *Harvard Business Review*. See https://hbr.org/2005/04/the-quest-for-customer-focus.

13. HubSpot describes its experience with reducing email frequency in "6 Marketing Lessons HubSpot Learned in 2017," by Jon Dick, January 16, 2018, in Thinkgrowth.org. See https://thinkgrowth.org/6-marketing-lessons-hubspot-learned-in-2017-b7013fc12059.

CHAPTER 9

1. SWOT stands for strengths, weaknesses, opportunities, threats. PEST analysis examines political, economic, social, and technological factors. Porter's five forces analyze competitors, suppliers, buyers, and the threats from new entrants and substitutes. Strategists use all of these frameworks to evaluate a company's evolving position in a competitive market.

2. Gartner describes the value of data assets in the Gartner Report "Why and How to Measure the Value of Your Information Assets," by Douglas Laney, August 4, 2016, refreshed on November 15, 2016. See https://www.gartner.com/doc/3106719/measure-value-information-assets.

3. For more on two-speed marketing, review Gartner's "Implementing a Two-Speed Marketing Program," by Heather Pemberton Levy, May 14, 2015, in *Smarter With Gartner*. See https://www.gartner.com/smarterwithgartner/implementing-a-two-speed-marketing-program/

4. More detail on how Farmers Insurance maximizes lifetime value is in "Implementing a Customer Lifetime Value Approach to Sales and Marketing Strategies," by Frost & Sullivan. See https://www.frost.com/prod/servlet/cpo/237680983.

5. For more on the capability maturity model, see "What is the Capability Maturity Model," by Select Business Solutions. See http://www.selectbs.com/process-maturity/what-is-the-capability-maturity-model.

CHAPTER 10

1. More detail on the retail apocalypse in "The Long and Painful Decline of the Retail Store," by Dwyer Gunn, April 11, 2017, *Pacific Standard*. See https://psmag.com/news/the-long-and-painful-decline-of-the-retail-store.

2. Amazon uses customer data in its advertising business, as described in "Amazon's Advertising Business Rumbles On," by Robert Elder, April 11, 2017, in *Business Insider*. See http://www.businessinsider.com/amazons-advertising-business-rumbles-on-2017-4.

3. Some are beginning to raise privacy questions about Google, as described in "Google goes for the wow at I/O, but what about privacy?" by Richard Nieva, May 10, 2018, in c|net. See https://www.cnet.com/news/google-goes-for-the-wow-at-io-2018-but-what-about-privacy-ai-virtual-assistant/

4. China's use of social evaluation for its citizens is from "China's Social Credit System puts its people under pressure to be model citizens," by Meg Jing Zeng, January 23, 2018, in *The Conversation*. See http://theconversation.com/chinas-social-credit-system-puts-its-people-under-pressure-to-be-model-citizens-89963.

INDEX

# #

A

B

C

D

E

F

G

H

N

O

P

Q

R

S

T

U

V

W

X

Y

Z